D1571727

THE WAY OF THE PATHANS

THE WAY
OF THE PATHANS

by

JAMES W. SPAIN

KARACHI
OXFORD UNIVERSITY PRESS
LONDON   NEW YORK

Oxford University Press, Ely House, London W.I

GLASGOW NEW YORK TORONTO MELBOURNE WELLINGTON
CAPE TOWN IBADAN NAIROBI DAR ES SALAAM LUSAKA ADDIS ABABA
DELHI BOMBAY CALCUTTA MADRAS KARACHI LAHORE DACCA
KUALA LUMPUR SINGAPORE HONG KONG TOKYO

P.O. Box 5093, I.I. Chundrigar Road, Karachi-2

First published in Great Britain 1962
Second edition printed in Pakistan 1972
Second impression 1973

Oxford University Press gratefully
acknowledges the permission of Robert Hale Limited,
the publishers of the first edition, to reproduce
the original setting of the text.

Printed by offset at
The Pakistan Herald Press, Haroon House, Dr. Ziauddin Ahmed Road,
Karachi.

To

EDITH

CONTENTS

ACKNOWLEDGEMENT

Quotations from Rudyard Kipling's poems, 'The Way of the Pathans', 'A Ballad of East and West', and 'The Lament of the Border Cattle Thief' (all of which appear in *Barrack Room Ballads*) are included by permission of Mrs George Bambridge, Messrs Methuen & Co. Ltd., and the Macmillan Company of Canada Ltd.

ILLUSTRATIONS

PREFACE TO THE SECOND EDITION

IT is now ten years since I wrote the preface to the original edition of this book. It is more than twenty since the episode with which the book begins took place. At that time I was a vice consul, the lowest of the low in the diplomatic business. When I last saw Peshawar on the same railway platform — in November 1969, I was Chargé d'Affaires of the U.S. Embassy in Pakistan.

Obviously, a fair amount of water had gone over the dam as far as I was concerned. But there are other more pertinent matters to consider. How had the Pathans and the Frontier fared in this score of years? Should I try to update my little book? Or leave it as a historical curiosity? And how much of it was still real anyway?

On reflection, I decided that enough of it was still real and that the best thing to do was to leave it alone. Great economic and social development have taken place within both Pakistan and Afghanistan. Political revisions have come — and some of them have gone again. International relationships have shifted.

But the book was never really about these things. It was about people and, insofar as I could discern, the well-springs of their lives and thought. These, I believe, have not changed. The friends I first made twenty years ago and now their children and grandchildren maintain the same traditions, the same individuality, and the same charm. *Pukhtunwali*, "the Way of the Pathans," is alive and well, and I am thankful for it.

I am more than ever thankful also to the people who first helped me with this book and to this day have continued to encourage my interest in the Pathans: my wife, Edith, who has followed me to many places since we first saw Peshawar together; Chaudri Mohammad Ali, Mohammad Aslam Khan Khattak, Khan Saadullah Khan, Mir Ajam, Khan Jamshed Khan Mohmand, Abdul Qadir Sehrai, and Miam Said Rasul.

Sadly, there are also those who have passed with the years: Ataullahjan Khan, Khan Abdus Satar Khan Mohmand, Abdur Rauf Khan, Abdur Rahim Khan, and A. K. Qureshi. Memories of them are fresh and I am sure that they too are happy that the way of life they knew still goes on.

Istanbul, July 1971.   J.W.S.

PREFACE

THIS frequently frivolous little book had its birth in an earlier, more sober work, my Ph.D. dissertation at Columbia University. When the last table and the final footnote were in place in the dissertation, I discovered I still had a supply of unrecorded anecdote and personal experience which promised to lend itself to a lighter volume of this kind. In addition, I had a collection of pictures, for which there seems to be no place these days in works with scholarly pretensions.

As it now develops, *The Way of the Pathans* will appear in print before the dissertation, which has been bogged down in the morass of academic publishing. I am not sorry, for my light-minded travelogue was more fun to write—and besides it may inspire at least a few persistent readers to look also at the other volume— when it finally appears.

When I wrote *The Way of the Pathans* I did not have a particular audience in mind, though, being an American, I suppose I assumed most of my readers would be the same. (A national characteristic, some might say!) Here again, however, events have had a way of directing their own course, and to my surprise and pleasure the book will be presented first to a British audience.

This inspires certain qualms. While British readers by virtue of long association with the Frontier can be assumed to be more familiar and more sympathetic to my subject, they can also be expected to be more critical—especially as far as the work of a newcomer is concerned. With this in mind, I pondered the desirability of going through the book with an eye to removing incidents or phrases which might be considered derogatory by a people whose connection with the Frontier is much older and more intimate than my own.

On second thought, I have decided to leave my account unchanged (with the exception of certain little conversions as of 'truck' to 'lorry' and 'honor' to 'honour'). For one thing, I think that the American point of view should in itself be interesting. For another, nothing was ever meant to be offensive, and if we have reached a point in social history where an author has to take special care not to offend the sensitivities of Britons, then, surely, there can be no subject left on earth which can be treated with casual frankness. Finally, of course, I have always expected to have to face the Pathans with what I have written, and, somehow, two formidable critics do not seem any more forbidding than one.

There remains only the obligation—and the pleasure—of expressing my gratitude to the large number of people who have helped me along 'The Way of the Pathans'. To name only a few: my wife, Edith, whose infrequent appearances in these pages are not indicative of the years of interest and experience we have shared on the Frontier, or her invaluable talent both for jogging my memory and editing its outpourings; His Excellency Mohammad Aslam Khan Khattak, formerly Pakistan's Ambassador in Baghdad, who helped awaken and direct my interest in his people; the late Khan Ataullahjan Khan, veteran of years in the Political Service; Abdus Satar Khan and Jamshed Khan, Mohmands, perennial hosts and my almost-brothers; the late Abdur Rauf Khan, Colonel Abdur Rahim Khan and Mir Ajam, splendid *raconteurs* of the ways of the Pathans; Abdul Qadir Sehrai, indispensable friend of every visitor to Peshawar; A. K. Qureshi and Mian Said Rasul, journalist and poet, and government officials both.

There are two other citizens of the Frontier, Chaudhri Mohammad Ali, long-time advocate-general in Peshawar, and now Vice-Chancellor of Peshawar University, and Khan Saadullah Khan, political agent and Commissioner, who deserve special thanks for their patience and helpfulness in answering my myriad questions and supplying some of the facts which have gone into these pages. Neither they, nor any of the others, can, of course, be held responsible for my judgements and opinions.

The latter is true also of the Ford Foundation, which financed my study and travel on the Frontier in 1953 and 1954, and of James Hurley of the School of Oriental and African Studies at the University of London, who made varied and vital contributions in the later stages of the work. Finally, there is Miss Sharon Volden, now of Augustana College, South Dakota, whose typing and grammatical skill gave the manuscript a considerably higher degree of respectability than it would otherwise have had.

                                                    J.W.S.

Washington, D.C. May 1962.

THE WAY OF THE PATHANS

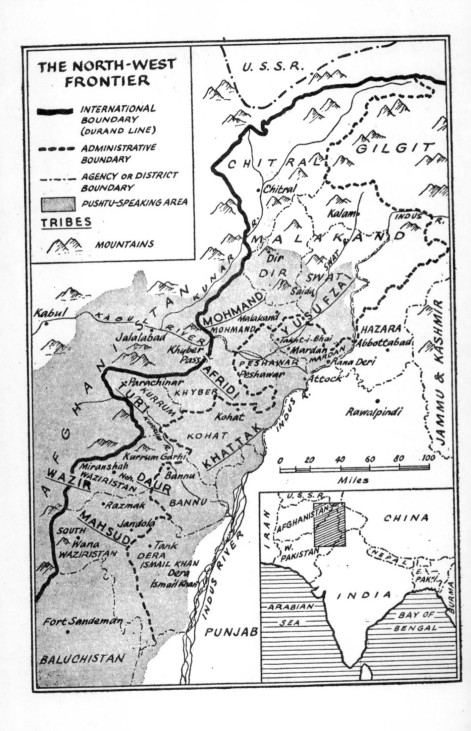

THE NORTH-WEST FRONTIER

INTERNATIONAL BOUNDARY (DURAND LINE)

ADMINISTRATIVE BOUNDARY

AGENCY OR DISTRICT BOUNDARY

PUSHTU-SPEAKING AREA

TRIBES

MOUNTAINS

U.S.S.R.

GILGIT

CHITRAL

Chitral

Kalam

MALAKAND

Dir

DIR

SWAT

Saidu

KUNAR R.

INDUS R.

Kabul

KABUL RIVER

Jalalabad

MOHMAND

MOHMAND

Malakand

YUSUFZAI

Takht-i-Bhai

Mardan

MARDAN

HAZARA

Abbottabad

Khyber Pass

PESHAWAR

Peshawar

Rana Deri

AFRIDI

Attock

Parachinar

KURRUM

KHYBER

KURRAM

Kohat

Rawalpindi

Kurram Garhi

KOHAT

KOHAT

INDUS R.

KHATTAK

Miranshah

WAZIRISTAN

Nth.

DAUR

Bannu

Razmak

BANNU

WAZIR

Jandola

SOUTH

Wana

WAZIRISTAN

MAHSUD

Tank

DERA ISMAIL KHAN

Dera Ismail Khan

AFGHANISTAN

Fort Sandeman

BALUCHISTAN

INDUS RIVER

PUNJAB

0   20   40   60   80   100

Miles

U.S.S.R.

IRAN

AFGHANISTAN

W. PAKISTAN

CHINA

NEPAL

ARABIAN SEA

INDIA

E. PAK.

BURMA

BAY OF BENGAL

JAMMU & KASHMIR

I

The Pathans and I

THE 'DOWN MAIL' on Pakistan's North-West Railway passes through Rawalpindi at 10 a.m. I arrived at the station at 1 a.m. with nothing to do but count the hours until the train came to take me back to my six-month-old job as vice-consul at the American Embassy in Karachi. At 2 a.m. I was squirming on a hard wooden bench in the 'First Class Retiring Room' when the 'up mail' came in. Eager for any diversion, I walked on to the platform to inspect it.

"Attock, Naoshera, Peshawar," the train guard offered. The names summoned up others in my mind: the Pathans, the Khyber Pass, Waziristan. On impulse I went back into the station and bought a ticket for Peshawar.

As the train ran through the dark countryside north and west of Rawalpindi, I remembered the first Pathan I had ever met. I was a boy of twelve. He was a gallant old outlaw named Kamal. A master of words named Rudyard Kipling brought us together:

Kamal is out with twenty men to raise the Borderside,
And he has lifted the Colonel's mare that is the Colonel's pride:
He has lifted her out of the stable-door between the dawn and
    the day,
And turned the calkins upon her feet, and ridden her far away.

I followed the story as the Colonel's son—he "that led a troop of the Guides"—rode forth to recover the mare. I held my breath as Kamal outrode, outshot, and disarmed the Colonel's son. I exulted when Kamal returned the mare and called forth his own son to ride back with the brave young Englishman. "Belike they will raise thee to Ressaldar," Kamal told his son, "when I am hanged in Peshawur."

It was some time, as a matter of fact, before I was even aware that Kamal was a Pathan. Kipling did not write for boys in the

15

American Mid-West in the Thirties, and the word 'Pathan' does not appear in 'The Ballad of East and West'. At first, I knew only that Kamal and his fellows were some unusual kind of Indians, rather like our own Indians of the American West, devoted to brave and warlike deeds. Later I came to know other characters: Mahbub Ali of 'The Ballad of the King's Jest' and *Kim*, Yar Khan of 'The Ballad of the King's Mercy', and the anonymous Afridi of 'The Lament of the Border Cattle Thief'. Then I began to have a dim idea of the great tribal brotherhood which sprawled across northern India and Afghanistan, encompassing such storied places as the Khyber Pass and the fabulous city of Peshawar.

Even when I came to Karachi, Kamal and Mahbub Ali remained sunk in my subconscious mind. The Frontier was a thousand miles away and I had other things to worry about. My job was to set up the Fulbright Foundation in Pakistan and get a programme of teacher and student exchange under way. One of the first Americans to arrive was a high-school teacher from Ohio, slated for a year at a select boys' school in the Murree Hills on the border of the Punjab and the North-West Frontier Province.

I decided to give myself my first excursion in Pakistan and personally take the teacher to his school. We descended on—or rather, ascended to—the hill school, and the principal, an Englishman of some twenty years' tenure, made us welcome. After dinner over the coffee I met my Pathans again, and Kamal and Mahbub Ali came galloping up across the years.

"I want you to see what one of my Pathan boys brought me back as a gift after the holiday," the principal said. "I'm going to send it up to the sisters at the convent tomorrow, but it really has quite a story."

A servant brought in an elaborate vestment of brocade and gold. It was a cope, marked with the liturgical symbols of the cross, the lamb, and the fish, and used in solemn Roman Catholic ceremonies.

"The boy is the son of an important chief," our host explained. "He brought this for me to make into a dressing-gown. It came from Baramula."

"Baramula?" I inquired.

"At the entrance to the Vale of Kashmir," the principal explained. "There's a fair-sized Catholic mission there. When the tribes were on the Kashmir *jihad* in 1947, they went through there. The wilder ones made quite a mess, I'm afraid, before their chiefs came up. A couple of nuns, also an English colonel and his wife, who were staying there, were killed in the first rush. This thing must have been down in Waziristan ever since. The boy who brought it is a fine lad," he explained to his new staff member. "You'll have him in your class."

After helping the new teacher check the heavy iron bars which protected his bedroom window, I said goodbye and took the nine o'clock bus down to the railway station at Rawalpindi.

The sun rose up as the 'up mail' curled around the ramparts of Akbar's weatherbeaten fort and rattled over the railway bridge across the Indus River at Attock. On the other side, village after village flashed by as we rode up the Peshawar Valley. Each was the same, a cluster of adobe houses surrounded by a blank brown wall. Narrow-slotted towers guarded the corners. A square inner keep dominated the whole. Behind the villages on each side was a rim of hills, rough and brown. On the north side, beyond the hills, a thin white line, cold, fragile and incredibly high, marked the Himalayas. As my eyes grew used to the glare of the sun on adobe, I saw turbaned figures. The third one I noticed, and then nearly every one after him, had a rifle slung on his shoulders.

The railway station of Peshawar Cantonment was something of a disappointment. It had a crisp, military look about it all right: a long shining platform, square, whitewashed stone buildings, precise flower beds. The only humans in sight were three slight brown men, one scrubbing down the platform, one poking a long-nosed watering-can into the flowers, the third uncertainly taking charge of my small bag.

Among them—and it took all three to achieve it—they got me to Dean's Hotel, a few streets away. Having had breakfast (choice of kippers or kidneys) at this storied hostelry under a full-length lithograph of a young King George VI, I was taken in tow by a fat and garrulous tonga-driver. In exchange for ten rupees and a promise of obedience to his selection of sights to be seen, I was to receive a morning's trot around Peshawar. I feared I had met my first Pathan, and I was not impressed.

From the bobbing back seat of the high-wheeled vehicle I saw the Club, the Anglican church, the Combined Military Hospital, Edwardes College, Government House, Sir George Roos-Keppel's house and the military farm—"all built by British people, sar, very good people, sar. You are British, sar? My friend have good shop here; we go visit him now—yes, sar?"

We didn't, but only because I was sure that there must be something more to Peshawar than this broad deserted avenue bordered by shade trees, clipped lawns, and solid Victorian bungalows. The shades of Kamal and Mahbub Ali certainly did not wander here.

"Bazaar . . . mosque . . . caravanserai . . . city . . . old city," I tried.

"City five rupees extra, sar—not worth it. City no good, sar—very uncivilised place."

"City!" I insisted.

My guide shrugged and we clattered down the Mall again. Near its end we turned off and rode along the railway tracks. In a few minutes the tonga lurched up a steep bridge, through a gap in a barbed-wire barrier, and down into a long narrow street.

"Kissakhani: 'Story-tellers' Street' they call it," the tonga-driver explained. He spat over his shoulder amid the crowd which teemed about us, and gave his panting horse a vicious cut with the whip. At the end of the street he pulled up. "You want to go farther, you walk," he instructed. "Nothing there but Pathans, always fighting, always killing, no good."

"You're not a Pathan?" I asked, trying to keep the relief out of my voice.

He shook his head in disgust at my ignorance. "No, sar. I civilised man. You pay me fifteen rupees now. You come back, I take you hotel free."

Not sure whether this was a bonus or a benediction, I paid and pushed my way into the city. I was unlimbering my camera in the coppersmiths' bazaar when I saw two young men walking through the crowd with an arrogant lilt, hand in hand, indifferent to the people opening a path for them. I turned with my camera and met my first Pathans.

Gesturing at the camera, I tried to make my intentions clear. They stood shoulder to shoulder, serene but uncomprehending. Bazaar hangers-on gathered around and I was pushed chest-to-chest with the tribesmen. In the whirlpool of smells that is the Peshawar bazaar, I was aware of the odour of salt sweat and warm cosmoline underlaid with sandalwood.

The tribesmen's gilt-painted basket turbans were wrapped about with blue and white cloths. Bandoliers fitted with polished brass cartridges crossed on their chests. Their eye sockets were darkened into black hollows with *kohl*. Each carried a slung ·303 Enfield rifle.

The traditional Islamic prohibition of graphic representation of the human figure occurred to me. However, we were now jammed too close together for me to use my camera. The same was true, I noted happily, of their rifles. Someone in the crowd passed a remark in a raucous voice. Obviously directed at my discomfiture, it drew a snicker from the by-standers. The older of the tribesmen (perhaps twenty-two) turned cold eyes on the speaker. He held up his hand and silence fell. I expected a speech, but after a moment he dropped his arm again, and we all waited.

Relief came as a slender youth dressed in a blue blazer, grey slacks, and tennis shoes wormed his way into the centre of the human knot. "Is something the matter?" he inquired. I explained my innocent purpose. He directed a rapid fire of Pushtu at the tribesmen. Without moving an inch from where they stood, they drew themselves even more erect. The crowd fell back. "Go ahead, sir, they are ready," said my interpreter. As I looked down into the viewer of my reflex, the older of the tribesmen, with a gesture worthy of the most accomplished actor, turned his head slightly, so that his classic profile with its great hawk nose came clearly into view.

Introductions followed. My rescuer said his name was Jamshed. His appearance had been accidental. He presented Ahmad Khan and Yusuf Khan, Afridis. I stuck out my hand. Ahmad shook it long and gave it up with seeming reluctance. Yusuf took it and held it in both his own, while Jamshed spoke at length. When he was finished Yusuf nodded solemnly. He said perhaps a dozen words in return. With a half-salute both men strode away.

Jamshed stood me to a cup of green tea at a nearby stall. He was, I learned, a graduate of the very school I had left a dozen hours earlier. The tribesmen were Afridis of the Kuki Khel, down for a day in town. Uneducated men, but good fellows not with-standing, said Jamshed.

"They don't seem to speak much," I ventured.

"They are young men. You should hear their father who is a very important *malik*," said Jamshed, calling for another pot of tea.

After a quick round of the Chowk Yad Gar, the central square of the old city of Peshawar, a scramble up the narrow Street of the Silversmiths, and a dash into the mosque of Mahabat Khan—where, Jamshed pointed out, the Sikhs used to hang true believers from the minarets—I was delivered back to the hotel by foot. My suggestions that we pick up the waiting tonga were over-ridden. "I know that fat Punjabi," said Jamshed. "He is a snake. I will go to him and tell him you have been killed in the city by a *badmash*. He will go to the police who will beat him, first for negligence and then for giving false information."

A little later, my first twelve-hour visit to Peshawar over, I boarded the 'down mail' to Karachi. The ghosts of Kamal and Mahbub Ali, nodding benignly in the smoky twilight, saw me off.

II

The Pathan Borderland

THUS BEGAN my active pursuit of the Pathans. I have been at it ever since and the subject has never palled. First, I looked for books that would tell me about the tribesmen of the North. But Karachi, a few years after the Partition, was not a library centre. So I had an excuse to return to the Frontier. During my remaining two years at the Embassy I made the journey six times. The American Fulbright grantees at schools in other parts of Pakistan began to feel that their situations could not be too bad. They never saw the cultural affairs officer. He was always taking care of some urgent problem in Peshawar.

I began to make Pathan friends. They ranged from assorted tonga-drivers in Peshawar (real Pathan tonga-drivers) to the Chief Minister of the Frontier Province.

There were Pathans in Karachi, following a variety of trades and professions. Our new American neighbours hired a Pathan cook, large, bearded, and devoted to American cake mixes. He was an excellent cook, but one morning broke down the kitchen door which had been insultingly locked against him. A democratic man, he always treated his employers as equals and his pride was hurt at what he considered suspicion.

Other Pathans came to the house in government cars and dinner jackets to present their own compliments and those of some Frontier acquaintance. Speaking with a casual, self-confident pride so enormous as to be appealing rather than repellent, they told me something of their land and their people.

Collecting bits and pieces of information was fine, but the desire to do a more thorough job persisted. While on home leave in 1953, I resigned from the Foreign Service and acquired a grant from the Ford Foundation. The grant gave me a year in New York, where at the Columbia University and New York Public Libraries I found the books, shelf after shelf of them. It gave me a summer in London where the archives of the India Office

Library and the Public Record Office yielded more treasures, and elderly Englishmen who had given much of their lives to service on the Frontier poured out their reminiscences. Most important of all, the Ford grant gave me six months back in the Frontier, during which time I was free to wander about, living in Pathan villages, trying to learn a bit of Pushtu, and checking the accounts of the libraries against the facts of the people.

The picture that emerged was fascinating. Including those who live in Pakistan and those who dwell in Afghanistan, there are about eleven million Pathans in all, give or take three or four million. The qualification must be added because no one has ever really counted them. The figures for tribal territory in the Pakistan Census are estimates, and anyone who knows how closely a Pathan guards his household and any secrets it may contain knows how rough the estimates must have been. In the case of Afghanistan, the figures are even less precise. The Afghan Government has claimed as many as seven million Pathans. Soviet writers (who are more and more in a position to know about things in Afghanistan) put the number as low as three million.

There are certainly almost twice as many Pathans as Kurds, which makes them the largest living tribal society in the World. They inhabit an area of more than 100,000 square miles, which is bisected by the Afghan-Pakistani border, almost inevitably called the Durand Line after Sir Mortimer Durand who in 1893 signed the agreement with the Afghan Amir Abdur Rahman which separated Afghanistan from India. The Pathans, incidentally, paid little attention to the international boundary then, and pay scarcely more today. Until a year ago when Pakistan closed the border, more than 200,000 of the nomadic Ghilzai tribe migrated annually from the Afghan highlands down into the plains of Pakistan. Perhaps as many non-nomadic tribesmen cross back and forth over the line casually each year as they go about their private business.

This business sometimes takes them far afield. You will find Pathans all over Pakistan and India. They man coastal vessels between obscure Indian Ocean ports, they serve as police officers in East Bengal, household servants in Bombay and New Delhi, customs agents on the Malabar Coast, gun-runners in Kashmir, and bank guards in Benares. In past centuries they have founded dozens of little princely states all over India. For a hundred years there has been scarcely a village in all of the subcontinent that did not know the Pathan money-lender, with his bag of coins, his long knife, his wicked smile, and his interest rates ranging upwards from fifty per cent a month.

There are second and third generation Pathans throughout South-East Asia. There is a Pathan colony in Australia. Some of the most prosperous farmers in California's rich valleys were born along the stony flanks of the Khyber Hills. There is more than one little Giovanni Khan in sunny Italian villages which their fathers first saw in the battle heat of the Second World War. In the Twenties, one of the first graduates of the notorious Communist University of the Toilers of the East in Moscow was a Pathan, and there are others scattered throughout the Communist world today.

Most Pathans, however, love their own barren hills with so fierce a passion that they do not leave them. Some men in their seventies have never left the boundaries of the land held by their own clan. Many have never gone beyond the limits of the Pushtu-speaking area.

The last thing a Pathan would call himself is 'Pathan'. Though the word is in common use in the West today, it is a Hindi form employed by the people of India to designate their fierce neighbours west of the Indus River. It was taken over by the British, and in the mouths of generations of Tommies was corrupted to 'Paythan'. Most of the tribesmen themselves use 'Pukhtun' or 'Pushtun' (the former in the guttural language of the northern tribes; the latter in the softer southern dialect). Some prefer 'Afghan', which in their case has nothing to do with Afghan nationality. All of these words are from the common language of the tribes: Pukhtu, Pushtu, or Afghan—depending on the accent of the speaker; it is an eastern Iranian dialect of considerable scope and antiquity.

The Pathans are divided into several dozen separate tribes, numbering from a few thousand to a few hundred thousand each. The tribes are in turn divided into *khels*, which may be roughly equated with clans. The *khels* break down into family systems of varying sizes and complexity. All are theoretically related to each other through descent from a common ancestor. Unfortunately, the relationship between the various units of Pathan society is infinitely complicated. Some *khels* are larger than tribes and have lost all practical connection with the parent group. The same name may be used by *khels* of different tribes. Distinctions which are very acute in one area are ignored in another.

Those who are less particular about such things than the Pathans themselves may distinguish four main groups, two based in Afghanistan and two in Pakistan. Of the former, the great Durrani tribe, which has traditionally supplied the royal family of Afghanistan, are the most important historically. They live in the middle and lower reaches of the Helmand River Valley and Kandahar has long been their capital. Many of them have become Iranianised over the centuries, and have all but lost command of their native Pushtu.

The other group which could, if it cared about such things, claim Afghan nationality, is the Ghilzai. The Ghilzai are the only true nomads among the Pathans. They summer in the Afghan highlands and winter in Pakistan. Whole villages and tribes move together, and two hundred thousand or so pass back and forth across the Durand Line each year. In Pakistan, they are known simply as *powendas*, 'nomads'. In Afghanistan the word *kūchi* is more frequently used to describe them. They themselves use the names of the dozen or so *khels* into which they are divided, the Suleiman Khel, the Ali Khel, the Aka Khel, etc. Each one of these has a 'home' area in the highlands between the Hazarajat of Central Afghanistan and the Suleiman Hills which mark the border with Pakistan, but its members wander as far westward as Herat, and in the old days roamed at least as far east as Bengal.

The third major grouping of Pathans is traditionally referred to as the 'independent' or 'free' tribes. These dwell in and around the Suleiman Mountains athwart the Durand Line. Some of the tribes are wholly within Afghanistan; some wholly within Pakistan; and some have members in both countries. Their tribal structure is more highly developed and better preserved than that of the other groups. They are known by their individual tribal names: Yusufzais, Mohmands, Afridis, Shinwaris, Orakzais, Bangash, Zaimusht, Wazirs, Mahsuds, and a score of others.

In Pakistan, most of them live in tribal territory, a strip of land between the Durand Line and the administrative boundaries of the settled districts of what used to be the North-West Frontier Province. In most of this area the law of Pakistan does not apply and the tribesmen are free to rule themselves according to their own customs. The visitor enters the administered area only with the permission of the Pakistani authorities and the tribe into whose territory he passes.

A few of the 'free' tribes, mainly the Yusufzai and the Mohmands, have members living in the settled districts as well as in tribal territory. These, and the other tribes which dwell wholly within the settled districts, the Khattaks, Muhammadzai, and Bannuchis, for example, together with certain detribalised clans, constitute the fourth group of Pathans.

The last two groups are in many ways the most interesting. The 'free' tribes have preserved the original Pathan society virtually intact. They think of themselves as Afridis, Wazirs, Mahsuds, etc., and their first allegiance is inevitably to their own clan. They live according to their own law, called *Pukhtunwali*, 'the way of the Pathan'. Theirs is a rough and untrammelled democracy tempered only a little by the hereditary prestige of certain families and by the authority of their *maliks*, or chieftains, whose influence is based primarily on personal bravery, wisdom, and strength.

The Pathans in the settled districts retain their language and culture and a keen sense of their identity, although their tribal ties have been weakened by a hundred years of close contact with the laws and manners of the British and the other peoples of Pakistan and India. Some of them are sophisticated and highly educated. It is from this group that most of the well-known Pathans of today come: General Ayub Khan, president of Pakistan; Abdul Qaiyum Khan, former chief minister of the North-West Frontier Province; Abdul Ghaffar Khan, 'the Frontier Gandhi', who played a large rôle in the fight for independence from the British and who has been a thorn in the side of every Pakistani Government since independence was achieved.

Politically, the tribal territory is divided into six agencies, each headed by a political agent who reports to the local divisional commissioner (at Peshawar and Dera Ismail Khan) and to the Ministry of States and Frontier Regions of the Central Government. The political agent's job has been aptly described as 'half-ambassador and half-governor'. The political agent for the Malakand Agency lives at Malakand in the north. The agents for the Khyber and Mohmand Agencies reside in Peshawar; for

Kurrum in Parachinar; for North Waziristan in Miranshah; and for South Waziristan in Wana.

The 'settled' districts constituted the North-West Frontier Province until 1955, when they were amalgamated with Sind, the Punjab and Baluchistan into 'one unit', the province of West Pakistan. West of the Indus are the districts of Peshawar, Mardan, Kohat, Bannu and Dera Ismail Khan. The overwhelming majority of their inhabitants are Pathans. Hazara District on the east bank of the Indus has a large number of non-Pathans, but it has been tied for so long to the others that it has come to share their Pathan outlook.

III

History and Legend

THE PATHANS are an ancient people, though perhaps not quite so ancient as they like to claim.

One day while lunching with a Yusufzai khan in the palm-shadowed garden of his house, I asked about the family ancestors.

The khan was preoccupied with a new automatic pistol he had just received from Spain. He worked the mechanism and sighted the weapon at the battlements of the surrounding court. I suspected he was fighting back the impulse to let go a burst. I also had a feeling it might not be good form to interrogate so blue-blooded a figure about his forebears. Nonetheless, he dispatched a retainer to the family archives and a few minutes later a list of several pages was put into my hands.

The genealogy ran in reverse order. At the top I recognised the name of my host's father with the titles Major-General, Nawab, Sir. Below this were two or three more names with British-conferred titles, Lieutenant-Colonel, Khan Bahadur, and the like. Then the names streamed backward, simple and un-adorned, page after page. Towards the end, they read like a roster of the great men of Israel: Suleiman ibn Daud, Irmia ibn Sarub, Yusuf ibn Yakub, Isat ibn Ibrahim. At the very end was Adam, a common Pathan name even today.

I did not pursue the subject further with the khan, who at the moment was more interested in his machine pistol. Some time later, several score miles away, in a Mohmand village, I reopened the question of Pathan origins. An old man, illiterate but widely respected for his knowledge of tribal lore, reeled off the names of the progenitors of the Mohmands, while I studied the Yusufzai khan's list. Sure enough, the two genealogies eventually came together with the name of Kand, the son of Kharshaban, son of Sarban, the son of Kais or Abdur Rashid, patriarch of all the

27

Pathans. Still later, two hundred miles farther south, the list of names recited for me by a Wazir elder was woven into the tapestry through Suleiman, son of Kakai, son of Ghurghusht, son of the same Kais.

Among the musty volumes of the India Office Library in London I found that dozens of nineteenth-century Englishmen had revelled in the discovery of the Pathans as a tribe of Israel. Kais, they expounded, was a chief of the seventh century AD, the thirty-fifth lineal descendant of Afghana, son of Jeremiah, son of Saul, first king of Israel.

The early Englishmen, many of them able although amateur scholars, had been as impressed as I was by the remarkable consistency of the genealogies they found among the Pathan tribes, and most of them were convinced that the Pathans' story of their origins was true. A few of the Britishers, indeed, even found a kinship with the Pathans by way of fantastic theories involving the descent of the original inhabitants of the British Isles from the 'lost tribes' of Israel.

The idea that the Pathans were descended from the nation of Israel was encouraged by their tight tribal structure, their stark code of behaviour, their strikingly Semitic features, their bearded patriarchal appearances, and their predilection for biblical names (acquired from the Holy Koran): Adam, Ibrahim, Musa, Daud, Suleiman, Yakub, Yusuf, Isa, and the rest. It was a favourite subject of speculation by British soldiers, administrators, and missionaries, and persisted in memoirs and travel books well into the twentieth century.

The only trouble is that it was not true. I feel something of a coward saying this here in a book written half a world away from the Frontier, when I know that I would never have the courage to say it to a Pathan.

Nevertheless, we must face the facts, although, happily, the facts about the Pathans are anything but prosaic. The myth of the Semitic origins of the Pathans was debunked more than a hundred years ago by Bernhard Dorn, Professor of Oriental Literature at the Russian university of Kharkov, in a book with the interesting title, *A Chrestomathy of the Pushtu or Afghan Language*, which was published by the Imperial Academy in Saint Petersburg in 1847. The most recent and comprehensive treatment of the subject appears in *The Pathans* by Sir Olaf Caroe, a former

British governor of the North-West Frontier Province (Saint Martin's Press, New York, 1958).

This is not to say that the genealogies should be ignored or taken lightly. They were first set down by Persian-speaking chroniclers at the court of the Mogul emperors in the early part of the seventeenth century. The sophisticated Mogul historians, possibly impressed by the same outward signs of Semitic connections that misled the British two hundred years later, apparently made up the descent of the border tribes from the mythical Kais and improvised a connection for Kais with Saul of Israel.

The Mogul historians, however, had a pretty good idea of the tribes and chiefs who existed in their time and the few generations preceding them. This they set down, providing us with an accurate outline of the Pathan clan structure three hundred years ago. The tribes made the genealogies their own and have preserved and kept them up to date religiously ever since. Thus the genealogies provide a reliable outline of the development and interrelations of the various clans over the past three hundred years.

The scanty historical information we have about the history of the Pathans is no less fascinating (and only slightly less subject to controversy) than that provided by the genealogies.

The Greek historian Herodotus refers to 'the most warlike of all the Indians, who live around the city of Kaspaturos in the country of Paktuike', and to 'the Aparutai', who lived in the seventh satrapy of Darius the Great of Persia. Sir Olaf Caroe unhesitatingly identifies Kaspaturos with Peshawar, Paktuike with the Pukhtuns or Pathans, and Aparutai with the Afridis.

Arrian, the chronicler of Alexander the Great's invasion of India, describes the places visited by the Macedonian in 327 BC after he had brought his armies across the Hindu Kush and before he had crossed the Indus. Several of them are clearly identifiable to anyone with a knowledge of Frontier geography.

The vestiges of the Greek civilisation established on the Frontier by Alexander and his successor were fairly quickly absorbed by the Indian Hindu-turned-Buddhist Mauryan dynasty which in the third and second centuries before the Christian era gave impetus to the Graeco-Buddhist culture known as Gandhara, the remains of which litter the Frontier area today. For the next thousand years, there is little history beyond the lists of Central Asian tribes—the Parthians, the Sakas, the Yueh-Chi, the Kushans, and the White Huns or Epthelites, who poured down upon the Frontier.

Towards the end of the tenth century the Frontier tribes appear again in history. They had already been converted to Islam, and many of them joined the ranks of the famous Mahmud of Ghazni, 'the Idol-breaker', when he began his long series of raids from his capital at Ghazni (just across the present Pakistan-Afghanistan border) into Hindu India in 1001. Mahmud, himself, was a Turk. It was in his time that the name 'Afghan' was first applied to the hill tribes.

In 1221 Jenghis Khan led his Mongols down into the Peshawar Valley in pursuit of a fleeing king of Iran. (Tradition has it that the Great Khan was five days behind his enemy at Kabul and only half a day behind at Naoshera.) One hundred and seventy-five years later Jenghis' descendant, Timur the Lame—called Tamerlane, left Samarkand to invade India. On his way back from Delhi, Timur's passage was made difficult by the Afghan tribes, who had now moved down from their hills and established forts in the area around Kohat and Bannu. Taking advantage of the chaos left in India by Timur, an Afghan chief, Bahlol Lodi, led his men all the way to Delhi and founded a dynasty there which lasted for seventy-five years.

When a descendant of both Jenghis Khan and Timur, Babur, the founder of the Mogul empire of India, launched his first invasion of the subcontinent from Farghana in Central Asia in 1505, the great divisions among the tribes had already become established and they occupied most of the area in which they are found today.

Their racial composition, then and now, is less than clear. The tribes who dwelled in the Frontier area in the days of the Greek historians were almost certainly part of the great Aryan horde which had moved down from Central Asia a millennium earlier. With their blood was mingled that of later invaders from the same area. In his memoirs, called the *Babur-Nama*, the witty and sophisticated Babur describes tribal attacks on his army as 'death-defying'. He also tells how some of them, after being defeated in battle, came to him with grass between their teeth proclaiming themselves his 'cows'. This act is familiar to the Frontier tribesmen today and represents the ultimate humiliation. Babur recounts with pride how he erected great pillars of the skulls of his fallen foes at Kohat, at Hangu, and in Bajaur. He describes how he took the daughter of a Yusufzai chief, Bibi Mubaraka, as a wife, how he hunted rhinoceros, and how he killed a tiger near the Indus above Attock.

For the next two hundred years the Pathans fought the Moguls. The chronicles of the emperors of Delhi are as full of accounts of Frontier revolts and unsuccessful punitive expeditions as are the archives of the British India Office in London. Many historians say that the Mogul empire in India began to wither when it was cut off from its tap roots in Central Asia. If this is true, the Pathans can claim no small share in bringing the mighty Moguls down.

The Pathans also profited from the chaos which accompanied the breakdown of Mogul power. Many Pathans served in the armies of the Persian Nadir Shah who in 1739 looted Delhi of its famed Peacock Throne. In 1761 a Pathan army led by Ahmad Shah Abdali, himself a Pathan, defeated the Mahrattas who had succeeded to the Mogul power in northern India at Panipat, near Delhi, and paved the way for the British conquest.

The Pathans had two more great battles to fight, and they still cherish the memories of them. The first was with the Sikhs; the second, with the British. The Pathans can hardly be said to have won either, since an alien flag flew over Peshawar from 1823, when the great Sikh maharaja Ranjit Singh took sovereignty over the city, to 1947, when the Union Jack was lowered for the last time in front of Government House. Still, neither the Sikhs nor the British could ever claim to have conquered fully, for the Pathans never ceased fighting. Then, as now, they found the prospect of another round with an ancient enemy only slightly less satisfying than a decisive victory in the first place.

Spreading out from their base on the Punjab, the Sikhs came first to Peshawar, to extort the gift of a prize thoroughbred from the Afghan governor. They stayed to oppress the inhabitants and to turn the countryside round about the city into a desolate wasteland. Their memory lives even today in the phrase 'Hari will get you!', which Pathan mothers use to frighten their children into good behaviour. 'Hari' is Hari Singh, one of the cruellest and most noted of the generals of the Sikh armies, a cosmopolitan company which included the Frenchman Ventura, the Italian Avitable, and the American Josiah Harlan. (Harlan, I am always proud to note to Pathan friends, spent only a brief period with the Sikhs before deserting to the service of the Afghan amirs of Kabul.)

The war with the Sikhs was a bitter and brutal affair, but it had a lighter side. An old Pathan gentleman told me the story of one battle which, he claimed, had taken place not far from his house. A Sikh army was encamped on the east bank of a stream, deterred by the swollen waters from attempting a crossing. On the west bank a group of Pathans rounded up some cows, animals sacred to the Sikhs as well as to the Hindus, and slaughtered them in full sight of the enemy. They then proceeded to cook and eat the cows. Goaded into action, the Sikhs sent infantrymen into the water. These were rapidly carried away by the rushing waters while the Pathans munched their *kebabs* and shouted insults.

Suddenly a band of Sikh cavalry swept from behind a patch of trees and galloped into the water. They struggled across before the feasting Pathans knew what was happening. "Then these fellows who had been eating so heartily," the old man told me with a chuckle, "were all killed, and so were all their kinsmen for a day's ride around."

In 1849 the Sikhs gave up dominion to the British. On the whole the Pathans appear to have welcomed the change, the British being less brutal and capricious than the Sikhs. They took care to respect the Pathans' Muslim beliefs and practices. In the eyes of the tribesmen they were no greater foreigners than the Sikhs, and indeed their Christianity was considered a little closer to the true religion than the essentially Hindu religion of the Sikhs. But what was most important was that, although the British collected taxes, they were prepared to provide subsidies to the tribes for good behaviour.

The British were also reasonable men, prepared to compromise when the occasion seemed appropriate. In the spring and summer of 1857 the notoriously unruly Zakka Khel Afridis made a series of raids upon British-administered territory around Peshawar. In the India Office Library in London I found the agreement which was signed with them to end this trouble. It was dated August 24, 1857, and Article 5 read: 'Reparation is *not* to be made in the event of any person of the tribe abducting the wife or daughter of a resident of British territory, but if he should have brought off any property also, that shall be returned.'

Perhaps the reason for this leniency in regard to Pathan peccadillos over women may be deduced from the date of the document. In August 1857 India was aflame with the sepoy Mutiny and Delhi was still in the hands of the rebels. The Mutiny had broken out in May at Meerut, and a few weeks later the two units of Bengal Native Infantry which were stationed on the Frontier refused to obey orders. Jittery British authorities in Lahore proposed to withdraw from the Frontier and concentrate their forces in the Punjab in an effort to check the rebellion. This proposal was overruled only at the last minute by the viceroy in Calcutta.

As it turned out, the breath of the Mutiny passed lightly over the Frontier. There were few, if any, Pathans in the British East India Company's army, and the hillmen considered the quarrel between the English and the sepoys none of their business. The mutinous units were easily brought under control and almost two hundred of their ranks blown from the mouths of cannon. The only British casualty was the colonel of the 55th Bengal Native Infantry, who blew his brains out in shame over the affair. The Afghan king, whom the British had been afraid would seize the opportunity to retake from the British the territory the Sikhs had taken from him, remained quietly in Kabul.

Having scorned to take advantage of the British while the Mutiny was on, the Pathans renewed their own battle almost immediately afterwards. Between 1858 and 1902 more than forty British expeditions had to take the field. The number of troops employed ranged from 280 (against the Utman Khel in 1878) to 40,000 (against the Afridis and Orakzais in 1897).

All this time, the British were tightening their grip on the Frontier. In the beginning they controlled only Peshawar, the main towns, and the roads which connected them. The main passes, including the Khyber, were still the domain of the hill tribes, some of which owed a tenuous allegiance to the amir of Afghanistan. As time went on the British introduced taxes and courts throughout the districts between the Indus River and the Border Hills. They then began to extend their influence up the passes, and during the Second Afghan War in 1878–1880 passed beyond to occupy for a brief time Kabul, Jelalabad, Ghazni and Kandahar.

The Pathans fought back on an *ad hoc* basis, killing a tax collector here, kidnapping a rich Hindu merchant there, and occasionally ambushing a British patrol. If anyone had told them that their freedom was in danger they would have laughed. The British sat in the towns, but they came into the hills seldom and at their own risk. If the Peshawar Valley prospered as never before, the caravans that came and went from it were richer, and the Pathans still took their ancient toll of them as they passed.

Towards the end of the century the situation changed. Tsarist Russia extended its power deep into Central Asia, dominating the ancient khanates of Bokhara, Samarkand and Khiva. British fears of the Russian threat to India mounted. 'The great game', of which Kipling tells so joyously, became a frantic scurry for advantage between two expanding empires. Peace and progress on the Frontier was of little concern to the men who ruled India. Security was the all-important objective. To this end, Afghanistan was looked upon as a buffer state. The settled Pathan districts along the Indus were made an integral part of India. Tribal territory in the hills was a marchland which must be dominated. The passes were occupied; new roads were built; forts were established and garrisons permanently stationed in them.

The Pathans' reaction was instinctive and violent. In the 1890s practically every tribe on the Frontier was up in arms at one time or another. Traditions of hospitality and sanctuary were violated as British civilians were ambushed and killed. The British replied in kind: tribesmen were transported to the Andaman Islands; villages and crops were burned; wells and fruit trees destroyed; and women and children starved by blockade.

The British won their security. They put down the risings. They held on to the passes and the roads, although they were never able to establish control over the hills. When it was over in 1901, Lord Curzon, recently appointed viceroy of India, formalised the new order by setting up a new province of India, the North-West Frontier Province, which included all the settled areas beyond the Indus, and by establishing a strip of tribal territory between the Province and Afghanistan which was directly under the control of the Government of India in Calcutta. At the same time the British lost whatever chance they might have had of winning the friendship and co-operation of the Pathans. The atmosphere of bitterness and revenge which was established at the turn of the century dominated relations with the tribes for the rest of the period of British rule.

This is enough history for our purpose here. The events which transpired between 1901 and 1947, the risings and reprisals, the bravery and treachery on both sides, can be found in other books; the full flavour of them can be had from the mouths of the old warriors (both British and Pathan) who lived them. In passing we need note only the irony of the fact that in 1901 British rule on the Frontier had already passed its half-way mark. It is safe to assume that the idea of the British one day leaving India never entered the wildest dreams of the ladies and gentlemen in the cantonments who toasted Curzon, the new viceroy, and Victoria, the old queen. They thought and acted as if they were to be there for ever.

IV

Peshawar

AS BEFITS a warrior tribesman, the Pathan is first of all a country-dweller. However, he has three cities, each in its way worthy of the title metropolis. In north-eastern Afghanistan, on the highway from South to Central Asia, Jelalabad sprawls among ancient shade trees. The city of 50,000 people lies in a fertile valley, dotted with orchards and crisscrossed with irrigation canals. Broken Buddhist *stupas* and still older remnants of the forts and towns of the Bactrian Greek civilisation founded by Alexander more than two thousand years ago lie up and down the valley and on the lower slopes of the tangle of mountains which stretches up into Badakhshan and Nuristan.

In south-eastern Afghanistan Kandahar nestles between the Tarnak and the Arghandeb Rivers, on the fringes of Baluchistan. It is the cultural heart of the southern Pathans, or Pushtuns, about 20,000 of whom dwell within and around its often-besieged walls. The country around Kandahar is the home of the Durranis, the ruling tribe of Afghanistan, who for centuries have supplied the dynasty which is enthroned in Kabul, the capital. Kabul itself is too far north and west to be part of the true Pathan country, though for centuries its destiny has been linked with that of the tribes, who have made and unmade kings with joyful contrariness.

Of the Pathan cities Peshawar is the unchallenged queen. Dubbed 'the Paris of the Pathans' by Lowell Thomas a quarter of a century ago, the ancient city has long been the focus of every hillman's delight. As late as 1930 it was the target of an Afridi attack, which all the military might of British India was barely able to contain. Some of the city gates still close at nightfall, not to open until dawn. Within them dwell more than 200,000 people, a melange which includes most of the races of Asia, and indeed of the other continents as well.

Peshawar has changed less than most cities over the centuries. The hill in the centre of the old city called the 'Gor Khatri' would probably still be remembered by the Chinese pilgrims, Fa Hien and Hiuen Tsang, who passed through in the fifth and seventh centuries AD. Timur-i-Lang the Mongol and Babur the Mogul would recognise it also. Most of the crumbling buildings on its top which now serve as a police station and land revenue office were built by the Sikhs when they ruled the city.

The Honourable Mountstuart Elphinstone, the first Englishman to visit Peshawar, in 1809, would have had no difficulty in finding his way about. In his day the city already numbered 100,000 inhabitants. The description Elphinstone set down of 'men of all nations and languages in every variety of dress and appearance' could be used today. The Peshawaris in 'white turbans, white and blue shirts, and sheepskin coats' are still there. So are the Persians and Afghans in 'brown woollen tunics and silk or sheepskin hats', the 'Khyberees with the straw sandals and the wild dress and air of their mountains', and the Hazaras, with their broad faces and little eyes, 'remarkable for their want of the beard which is the ornament of every other face in the city'. Just as a hundred and fifty years ago, there are still to be seen on the street only 'a few women with long white veils that reach their feet'.

The British took Peshawar's first census in 1868. The results intrigue the imagination. Thirty-one separate castes, tribes, and races were counted—including seventeen Americans. One wonders what those seventeen adventurous Yankees were doing so far from home only two years after the end of the American Civil War. Perhaps they were not Yankees at all. Perhaps they were defeated Confederates searching for relief from the despairing days of the Reconstruction. Maybe they were Irish insurgents seeking to frustrate Her Majesty Queen Victoria's justice by laying claim to another nationality. In any event, the dusty records tell no more about them than their presence.

The professions of the time were as colourful as the people. There were 1,425 police, 2,151 priests, 4 printers, 1 jeweller, 5 chemists, 2,411 blacksmiths, 1,701 goldsmiths, 4,806 beggars, 1,201 female musicians, 147 dancing girls, and 307 prostitutes.

Physically and geographically, Peshawar offers all the advantages that any man, Pathan or stranger, strategist or sybarite, could want. Situated a dozen miles from the entrance to the Khyber Pass, it is the north-western terminal for the subcontinent's railway system. For centuries it marked the end of the Grand Trunk Road across northern India, along which Kim and his lama wandered, and the end of the long caravan road from Persia, Turkistan and China. It lies athwart the north-south route between the Himalayas and the Salt and Suleiman ranges to the south. The entrance to the Persian Gulf, the southern half of Soviet Central Asia, western Tibet, and practically all of northern India lie within a thousand miles of the new jet runways at the Pakistani Air Force base on the outskirts of the city.

All the luxuries of the East are crowded together for sale in the bazaars that cluster about the central square of the old city: brightly painted china from the USSR, mellow carpets from dozens of cities whose names read like a litany from the golden age of Islam, precious metals and gems from all over Asia, the skins of rare beasts from the Himalayas, green tea from China, saffron from Kashmir, lush green melons from the Afghan highlands, blood oranges from nearby groves. Side-by-side with this exotic merchandise are the practical goods of the West: American tyres, German cameras, Czech rifles, Japanese radios, and British tweeds.

An air of expectancy pervades Peshawar, despite its many years. If the inhabitants appear to be ready for anything, they usually are. In 1946, when Jawaharlal Nehru came up from Delhi to plead for a united free India, they threw mud and more unpleasant things at him and chased him out of town. The next year many of them went off to Kashmir, where they created an international incident which still stirs the United Nations. In 1955, when an Afghan mob insulted the Pakistani Embassy in Kabul, they sacked the office of the Afghan consul in Peshawar and scattered his papers in the Kissakhani Bazaar.

On one visit I stood in the Chowk Yad Gar with a crowd watching a *hakim* demonstrating his medicines 'guaranteed to cure all the ills of man'. "The wise need not fear king cobra," proclaimed the *hakim*. "I offer you safety for life." He smeared a brown paste on his wrist and permitted a hooded serpent to strike him.

The crowd held its breath. One of its ragged members turned to pass a friendly remark: "The *hakim sahib* will not die, I think, but sometimes these doctors make mistakes and that would be well worth seeing."

Later I prowled among the ancient *serais* which nestle along the crumbling city walls. Once the great caravans from Bokhara, Samarkand, Herat, Meshed and Kashgar unloaded here. Now most of the *serais* are garages. In one I found a hint of former glory, a tattered snow-leopard skin hanging on the wall above a grimy timetable of the Afridi Bus Line. A twinkling-eyed old man, patching a tyre, explained: "A caravan brought it from the mountains of China when I was a boy. All that is over now," he added, "but it is no matter. Buses are much faster."

The Mahabat Khan Mosque is one of the true Peshawari's favourite sights. "The godless Sikhs when they ruled here hung true believers from its minarets," he tells you proudly, "two, every day." He is likely to add the names of those of his ancestors who achieved the distinction, saying "May peace be upon them."

The approach to the mosque is from the central square of the old city, the Chowk Yad Gar. The Street of the Silversmiths, a dozen feet wide at the most, winds up a steep hill. On both sides, three- and four-storey buildings exclude the sun, permitting only an occasional flash on the heavy necklaces, ear-rings and anklets which hang in the open shopfronts. Above is a narrow avenue of blue sky, winding up the hill in perfect parallel to the dark canyon of the street.

Half-way up the hill shining against the blue, brighter and purer than any bangle in the street below, hang the dazzling white minarets of Mahabat Khan. Beneath them, in the centre of a wide tiled court, is a pool, mysteriously clear and cool in the midst of the hot murky huddle of the city. Turbaned men, black-bearded, white-bearded, and red-bearded, move sedately about, stopping to kneel and bow in prayer on the rich red carpets that are scattered on the tiles. It is not difficult to understand how even the wildest young Afridi from the hills can find peace here.

A friend who was with me obtained permission from the *imam* of the mosque to ascend one of the minarets. From it we looked out over the city. Life was going on on the jumbled roofs and balconies spread out below us. A group of men drank tea and took their turn at the *chilum*, the simple Pathan hubble-bubble pipe. A knot of women squatted chattering as they sorted spices. The rapid beat of the little wooden mallets with which is made the silver foil that decorates sweets could be heard from a nearby balcony. The sound of a drum and the minor-key skirling of the Pathan pipes drifted from behind a half-closed lattice, through which swaying figures could be seen dimly. If one must be hanged, there could hardly be a more glorious scaffold, but it must have been doubly hard for a Pathan to choke out his life in sight and sound of all this.

The business streets of Peshawar are highly specialised. One is for shoes, another for headgear, yet another for cloth, a fourth for silver, a fifth for carpets, and so on for the seemingly infinite variety of goods which the city boasts. However, interspersed among all of them, so frequently as to appear to be virtually every other shop, are the tea-stalls.

Most of the tea-stalls are similar in appearance—perhaps six feet wide, of roughly the same depth, with a narrow ledge open to the street. Each has the same equipment: a large brass samovar, sometimes bearing the tsarist coat-of-arms, an iron or stone bed for piles of burning charcoal, and racks along both walls for cups and pots of red and blue china patterned after the famous Gardner china of imperial Russia. The proprietor sits cross-legged among his gear. His age may be eight or eighty, but his smile is the same.

The tea-shops cater for a variety of tastes. Some offer a strong black brew—as often as not 'English breakfast'—with a heavy dose of buffalo milk and semi-refined local sugar all boiled together. Others feature Kashmiri tea, in which the sugar is replaced with salt and the orange pekoe leaves with a particularly acrid variety of the plant. Most, however, serve only *qahwa*, the light, delicate Chinese green tea which is the Pathans' national beverage.

An Arab, to whom *qahwa* means coffee, would be surprised at the taste of the Peshawar product, but he would recognise in its making a ritual comparable to that of his own coffee hearth. First, a minute quantity of hot water is drawn from the samovar into a pot to warm it, and sometimes to clean it out as well. This is discarded. Then a tea-spoon or two of tea is spilled into the pot. Next, another few ounces of hot water are put in to 'wash' the tea. This is swirled off with grace and skill, and the process is repeated twice more. Then the pot is filled with boiling water from the samovar; a liberal helping of sugar is added, and the pot set on top of the glowing charcoal. While it is bubbling, the proprietor throws two or three cardamon seeds into a wooden pestle and crushes them. After a few minutes he removes the pot, sniffs the contents, and, if the scent is right, adds the crushed cardamon. The pot goes back on the coals for another minute or two. Then, after another discriminating sniff, it is presented with a cup on a tray to the customer. The price is from two to four *annas* (about as many pennies). There are few better bargains in the World.

The merchandise in Peshawar's bazaars is exotic, but transactions are down to earth. Prowling through the shoe-bazaar, I counted almost two dozen different varieties of shoes in one shop. These ranged from the narrow thin-soled 'Persian slipper' variety made of soft white leather embroidered with blue and gold to a massive pair of brogans of Dutch wooden-shoe design with soles fully two inches thick. I inquired about the special purposes of the different types of shoes and the cobbler was co-operative: "For wedding of very rich lady . . . for going to office . . . for soldier . . ." he explained. By the time I got to the brogans he sensed that he had a window-shopper and nothing more on his hands. "For walking to Kabul," he said. "You want to, Sahib?"

The street of the hardware merchants is not far from the shoe-bazaar and competes with it in the variety of its goods. Of these, the knives are the most interesting.

The Pathan makes his own knives, and like anyone else he likes to give them an extra touch. Many of the blades forged in and around Peshawar bear crudely stamped and often mis-spelled imprints: 'Best Sheffield Steel', 'Sharpest Stainest Steel', etc. There are small delicate pen-knives, worthy to grace a charm bracelet, and large switch blades which could hold their own in any bar-room brawl. The characteristic local dagger is bone-hilted, heavy-shafted, with a triangular blade designed to remain intact when it hits the bone. (Thus, the Pathans compete in practicality with the Gurkhas, who cut a small double notch into the blade of their *kukris* to deflect the blood coming down the blade from running on to the hilt and making it slippery to hold.)

One day I found a new item at my favourite shop. It consisted of a thin curving blade, four or five inches long, which folded back into a flat brass holder, both blade and holder in turn jack-knifing into a substantial bone hilt. The whole thing, when extended, was about eighteen inches long and looked like a miniature scythe. I took it into my hand and made a few passes at the ground with it. "For cutting corn?" I asked. The vendor took it back and, grinning, gestured with it at a higher level. "No, Sahib," he said, "for cutting faces."

One of the first things the British did when they settled down in India was to build 'cantonments' adjacent to the old cities which they used as administrative centres. In the cantonments were located the homes and offices of the British officials, military barracks, parade grounds and parks, churches and halls, hotels and Western-style shops. The street names were often reminiscent of nineteenth-century London, but the cantonments inevitably took on a local colour of their own.

The Peshawar cantonment is Victorian England with a rich Pathan flavour. It begins opposite the Kissakhani Bazaar, beyond the great round Sikh fort which is now the headquarters of Pakistan's Frontier Corps, and spreads out along both sides of the wide tree-lined Mall. High two-wheeled tongas, identical in design with those illustrated in early editions of Kipling's *Plain Tales from the Hills*, still trot past the green lawns which sweep up to Government House—once a scene of daily pomp and activity but now usually vacant.

Scattered here and there, far back from the streets, with walls three feet thick, ceilings fourteen feet high, and small deep-set windows not far below the ceilings (to make sniping difficult) are massive bungalows. Most have colourful local histories of their own. On the west side of the cantonment, with its back towards the Khyber and twin cannon at its front gates, is Roos-Keppel House, residence of the Political Agent for the Khyber. I have never passed it without seeing groups of Afridis drinking tea in the shade of the veranda, waiting their turn to tell their troubles to or make their demands upon the Political Agent. The picture has changed little in almost a century.

There is probably someone in Peshawar who knows how old Dean's Hotel is. However, the local management disdains to offer such information to the inquirer. One thing is sure. The sprawling, single-storey buildings laid out like an American motel over a three- or four-acre plot are always freshly painted, and hospitality is never held back. Also there are traditions. Even on the most sultry July evening, dinner proceeds majestically from soup (usually mulligatawny), to fish, to roast, to curry, to sweet. You always get three vegetables with the roast at Dean's, and more than once I have faced cauliflower prepared three different ways.

The register at Dean's, in which guests indicate the point from which they came and their destination and expected date of departure, is an invaluable aid for the motorless traveller seeking a ride to Rawalpindi, Kohat, Swat, or Kabul. The local wits say it is copied half a dozen times a day by representatives of as many intelligence services.

There are two museums in the cantonment. Both have been mellowed by time and the ghosts which stand in their shadowy corners are as gentle and benign as their originals were fierce and high-spirited.

In the Government-run Peshawar Museum, down by the cantonment railway station, the occasional tourist peers at trays of ancient coins bearing the likenesses of the petty Greek kings who ruled the Frontier in the wake of Alexander. Troops of schoolboys in grey cotton home-spun prance around the wooden horses which are the funereal effigies of the Kaffirs of Chitral. Both tourists and schoolboys are entertained and instructed by the curator, a local savant with the hawk nose and spade beard of an Assyrian king and a background of study at Harvard.

The images which decorate the walls of the privately-sponsored Peshawar Club up on the Mall are two millennia later in time than the silver kings and stone Buddhas of the museum. One group of them, the Masters of the Peshawar Vale Hunt, circles the dark-panelled walls of the main bar. The faces in the formal picture are strongly British. Even the few women who achieved the coveted MFH (Master of Fox Hounds) in the Thirties and Forties appear ruddy despite the faded brown and grey half-tones. When the ribbons flow from the chandeliers and the music of violins sounds through the Club, as it still does at the annual Christmas Ball, it is not difficult to imagine that the eyes in the pictures shine once again and even that the scarlet jackets sway to the waltz.

The cantonment has its own bazaar, called Saddar. Here the charm of the city is combined with the convenience of the Western-style shops along the Mall in an atmosphere which is very Pakistani. On one side of the main street is Green's Hotel which, for a modest sum, will provide at any hour of the day or night a chicken, split and broiled in a basting of spices that beggars description. Across the way is the solemn-fronted office of the *Khyber Mail*, the Frontier's leading and only English language newspaper in which debates in the UN and skirmishes on the Mohmand Border are featured side by side. Farther down is the carpet shop of Wazir Mohammad, where a long succession of American Fulbright grantees at Peshawar University have exchanged most of their monthly stipends for royal Bokharas and princely Khivas.

The university is perhaps the greatest achievement of Peshawar's twenty-odd centuries. When I first saw it in January of 1952 it was a single old building a few miles west of the cantonment on the road to the Khyber. I had come up from the American Embassy in Karachi to see what help the Fulbright Foundation —which was then in the same embryonic state as the university— might offer at an indefinite future date. An official of the Education Department told me that the Chief Minister, who was also chancellor of the university, would discuss the matter with me during his evening walk at the university site. "We have two streets laid out now," he told me, "and it is possible to walk even in the dark without falling into the mud."

The glow of the setting sun was still visible above the Khyber Hills when I arrived; it was not difficult to spot Khan Abdul Qaiyum Khan. Well over six feet in height and eighteen stone in weight, he was strolling along enveloped to his ankles in an enormous *chogha*, the loose woollen overcoat of Central Asia. At a discreet distance half a dozen guards armed with Sten guns moved with him.

He pointed at a low wall. "There is the foundation of the student's hostel," he said. "I laid the cornerstone three months ago. Each boy will have his own room." His arm swept in a circle. "The Engineering College will be there; the administration building, there; the law college on this side; the science faculty over here. The professors' bungalows will be back there. We will put guards on each house so that they need not be afraid. They will be needed in September. How many can you give me?"

I peered out across the empty plain and equivocated. "We will try to have them when you are ready for them—perhaps two or three. I will let you know when I return to Karachi."

The miracle of it was that by September the hostel was up and one hundred and fifty students were under its roof, each in his own room, an academic luxury virtually unknown in Asia. The first classes began in the engineering college as the masons took down their scaffolding. The plumbing in the professors' bungalows was connected the day they moved in. Since then buildings, student body and faculty have multiplied many times over, and the caravans of the *powenda* nomads coming down from the Khyber now pass through a scholarly community which can hold its own with all but a handful of the largest and most venerable of the European and American universities.

V

The Way of the Pathans

THE ROADS which lead out of Peshawar are among the city's most intriguing charms. To the west, the ancient highway to Central Asia passes through the cantonment, on out past the university, and within a dozen miles into the Khyber Pass. To the south the road climbs into the Kohat Pass, past the gun factories at Darra, and on down to Bannu, Tank, Dera Ismail Khan, Fort Sandeman and Quetta in Baluchistan. To the north lie Malakand, Swat and the great peaks of the Karakoram and the Pamir. To the east the Grand Trunk Road runs through Naoshera to Attock and the Indus.

Before taking to the roads and venturing out into tribal territory, we shall pause for a few pages to consider the things which govern life in the hills, where a Pathan is a Pathan and nothing else matters. Foremost of these is *Pukhtunwali*, 'the way of the Pathan', sometimes called the Pathan Code.

The first and greatest commandment of *Pukhtunwali* is *badal*, revenge. The obligation to take revenge for a wrong, real or fancied, falls not only upon the man who suffered it but also upon his family and his tribe. Neither the Law of Pakistan nor that of imperial Britain before her has ever held sway in the tribal territory. Hence revenge there is uninhibited and, since both insult and retaliation involve clans as well as individuals, the blood feud flourishes. Some feuds which are alive today were generations old when the Hatfields and the Coys exchanged their first shots.

The Pathans are proud and sensitive men; the number of things which they construe as insult or grievance are legion. Most frequently the trouble centres on *zar*, *zan* or *zamin*: gold, woman and land. Sometimes the feud grows out of an injury to a man's personal possessions, his family, or his land. Often it may begin over a negative act, the failure of one man to show as much respect for another's character or property as the latter feels is

46

Street of the Silversmiths with the Mahabat Khan Mosque, Peshawar

(*Left*) Copper bazaar, Peshawar

(*Below*) The mosque of the Islamia College, the University of Peshawar

his due. Once begun, the feud transcends the affair of the moment and spreads far and wide in time and space. Many an unexplained killing in Karachi, Singapore or London has had its origin a generation or two earlier in a remote village in the Khyber Hills.

All too often the feud ends only after one or both families are wiped out. Very rarely it may be terminated when the weaker party, in order to avoid extinction, throws itself upon the mercy of its enemy. This is called *nanawati*. It involves the ultimate humiliation. The appeaser goes with his women unveiled carrying the Koran upon their heads to offer a few sheep to his enemy and seek his pardon. More usually some sober third party, perhaps a neighbouring chief or the political agent, intervenes to settle the quarrel by mediation. In such an arrangement blood money may be accepted in lieu of revenge, and the honour of all concerned is satisfied. The effect of inflation is interesting to note in this regard. In the nineteenth century a life was usually worth 360 rupees. Today among the Mahsuds (who set a higher value than most other tribes) the figure is 7,700 rupees (£578).

The Pathans' second commandment is like to the first in the rigour of the obligations it imposes. However, *melmastia*, hospitality, is gentler in nature. In its most obvious form *melmastia* is implemented through the provision of food and lodging to the stranger or guest—or, indeed, even to an enemy if he should claim it. The lavishness of the hospitality varies according to the circumstances of the host. A poor villager will offer tea and stew up a few pieces of goat-meat. A wealthy chief will place his house and retainers at the guest's disposal and feast him with a whole sheep.

In any event the host, however distinguished a *malik* he may be, sits as an equal with his poorest guest and serves the meat with his own hands. But at the same time his influence is often reckoned by the number of people who come to him to share his hospitality, and the width of his *dustikar* (table cloth) usually indicates the importance of the man who spreads it.

The customs of the tribes extend into official circles. In Gilgit I remarked over lunch to the political agent that I had heard that the game of polo originated there. At three o'clock I was led to the place of honour, to watch a hastily arranged game between two units of the Gilgit Scouts.

On another occasion, I told a local army commander in Bannu

District that I had heard much about the Khattak dances which his troops had demonstrated at Government House in Peshawar on the previous Independence Day. While lingering over after-dinner coffee in the officer's garden that evening, three dozen twirling, shouting men, brandishing swords and torches in rhythmic frenzy, burst upon the scene, and executed half a dozen sets.

In Tank my wife mentioned the thrilling scenes of tent-pegging she had once seen in a film. She added that she remembered vividly the rows of horsemen sweeping down on wooden pegs set in the ground and plucking them up with their long lances. Tea that afternoon was served at the edge of the nearby athletic field. Her host, the political agent for South Waziristan, appeared in white drill and shining black boots. Having had his cup of tea, he mounted and rode off to join a group of army officers and tribal levies. A few moments later the horsemen thundered by, lances lowered for the pegs.

Melmastia also demands that the Pathan accord protection to his guest and to all who claim it from him. In this regard *melmastia* takes precedence over *badal*, and even the enemy who comes seeking refuge must be granted it and defended against his pursuers. This custom was a constant irritant in the Pathans' relations with the British in the old days. The man proclaimed a criminal in Peshawar could flee to the hills and could not only expect but demand protection and sanctuary from every house he came to.

A chief or a clan may accord general protection to a guest or stranger, undertaking to defend and be responsible for him while he is in the neighbourhood. This is frequently signified by the giving of one of the chief's possessions, a dagger or some article of dress. The token reminds all who see it that the honour of the protector is intimately associated with the well-being of him who carries it.

On one of my first visits to the Frontier a chieftain with whom I stayed insisted on giving me his *chogha*, the voluminous wool outercoat with embroidered collar and belt favoured by the Pathan gentry. It was cold and I wore it constantly while going about with him. I continued to use it for several days while I tarried in Peshawar, before returning to the hot plains of Karachi. It was not until several months later that I discovered that a pair of my host's retainers, whom I had noticed strolling about

Peshawar with uncommon frequency, had been kept busy for days seeing to it that no harm came to the stranger who so casually wore their master's honour about the city streets.

One of the main instruments for implementing *melmastia* on a day-to-day basis is the *hujra*, or guesthouse. This consists of a room or two where the visitor is quartered and fed. Each village will have one or sometimes two or more *hujras*. Most *maliks* and khans have their own.

In addition to serving as a headquarters for transients, the *hujra* is a kind of club for the local inhabitants. The men of the clan gather there to drink tea and discuss the affairs of the day. Many *hujras* now have a radio and the information provided by Radio Tashkent, the BBC and the Voice of America, as well as by Radio Kabul and Radio Pakistan, is digested and commented upon at the same time as the local gossip. The atmosphere is exclusively male, and frequently the bachelors of the household also sleep in the *hujra*.

The leaders of the Pathan clans are called *maliks*. In Arabic the word means king. A Pathan *malik*, however, is no more than a first among equals, and that only by dint of constant endeavour to prove that he merits his slight pre-eminence.

Any man who can inspire a handful of his fellows to accord him the right of leadership, however limited, is apt to be called *malik*. In most of the clans, however, the leading malikship is vested in a particular family. Primogeniture is not recognised and the mantle of leadership is accorded to the most capable and respected male within the family. Amongst the settled Pathans of the plains the title is usually khan.

Islam came to the Pathans earlier than to most other peoples of the subcontinent. Since the tenth century all of them have been Muslims. Most are of the Sunni persuasion, although there are pockets of Shias here and there. The mulla, or priest, plays an important rôle in their life. As is the case with other Muslims, the Pathans have no formally ordained clergy. Any man who feels the call to preach the word of God becomes a mulla. Most often, however, he comes from a mulla family, that is, one which has traditionally supplied the priest for a particular village or clan.

The warrior-bishop of the Middle Ages frequently finds his counterpart among the hill Pathans. Many of the most ferocious revolts against the British were led by mullas preaching *jihad* (holy war) against the government of unbelievers. The notorious Fakir of Ipi, who for thirty years defied first the British and then the Pakistani Governments from his cliffside headquarters in Waziristan, began his rise to fame when he inspired a tribal rising against a British court decision which demanded the return to her parents of a Hindu girl (renamed Islam Bibi) who had been kidnapped and married by a Pathan schoolmaster.

With the coming of Pakistan the 'infidel challenge' of the British vanished, though the mulla still is apt to oppose authority. He is violent in his denunciation of any modification of the secluded status of women. However, he usually can be kept under control and his activities turned into relatively constructive channels by a competent *malik*.

The *jirga* is probably the most interesting of all the Pathans' institutions. It can best be described as an assembly or a council, and it serves the functions of both. The word can be applied to half a dozen men sitting down together to discuss what they should say to the political agent who is coming to object to their sons shooting off the porcelain insulators from the nearby telegraph line.

More properly a *jirga* is a group of members of a particular sub-group of Pathans considering a matter of common interest. There is seldom any formal selection of representatives. Among some tribes virtually every adult male may attend. Among others tradition clearly indicates those who are entitled to participate. In any event there is no making of motions, and no voting. Decisions are unanimous and are arrived at by taking the 'sense of the meeting'. (Some of them would chill the blood of the peaceful Friends who coined the term.) The traditional penalty for anyone who defies the decision of a *jirga* is the burning of the culprit's house. Since the tribesmen do not lay aside their arms while deliberating, punishment can be executed promptly.

Apart from enforcing its own penalty for contempt, there is little of the judicial or police function in the *jirga*'s rôle in the community. It does not ordinarily determine guilt or inflict punishment but seeks to achieve a settlement. Both plaintiff and defendant appear before it as equals. If it cannot get them to agree to a settlement, for example, the acceptance of blood money in lieu of revenge for a death, it merely defines the rights of the parties concerned in accordance with established Pathan traditions.

The *jirga* has another function—in what might be called foreign affairs. It is the *jirga* which hears the political agent or a representative of another tribe who wishes to discuss a matter of mutual interest. Or the *jirga* may designate its own representatives to attend an inter-tribal *jirga*, to negotiate with the Government for a school or hospital, or to inform a distinguished foreign visitor of the tribes' impatience with the deadlock on Kashmir. Such representatives, unlike Burke's ideal member of Parliament, have no freedom, nor are they expected to use their own judgement or heed their own conscience. They are merely the instruments of the *jirga* and are bound by its instructions.

One cannot talk for long with a group of Pathans without the word *lashkar* coming into the conversation. Its closest English equivalent is probably the term 'war party', as it used to be used to refer to Indian bands in the American West. When a Pathan mentions a *lashkar* more often than not he is referring to the great Kashmir *lashkar* of 1947–1948 (sometimes called the Kashmir *jihad*). Tens of thousands of Pathans participated in the fighting in Kashmir. They were within five miles of the Srinagar airfield and would have taken it, and with it the whole of Kashmir, had they not stopped to enjoy their loot. During the course of one night the Indian Government managed to fly in a single company of Sikh soldiers who held the airfield until reinforcements came up by air from India.

The Kashmir *lashkar* is by no means the only source of battle stories among the Pathans. Practically every man in the hills has at one time or another participated in a battle against another tribe or clan. Many of the older men still tell of their exploits against the British—and one detects a gleam of envy in the eyes of the younger tribesmen as they listen.

The basic battle tactics of the *lashkar* are simple. Surprise is the major element. Ambush is a favourite way to achieve it. Direct attack on a fortified village is difficult and there are prescribed tactics for it. The classic *lashkar* is divided into three parts, one somewhat larger than the others. The larger party makes the assault, and having carried out its objective—the killing of an enemy, the burning of his house (or in local parlance merely 'the pulling of his beard')—retreats, probably laden with spoils.

About half-way back to its own village the assault party passes behind the protection of one of the smaller groups which have dug in to meet the inevitable pursuers. After a delaying action with the pursuing party, this group falls back to join the third stationed not far from the home village where another skirmish takes place. By this time the assault party is safe within its own walls and the others withdraw to join it. Then all turn to mock the pursuers from the vantage of the walls and turrets.

To the visitor with a historical or philosophical turn of mind, one of the most fascinating things about the tribal territory is that in much of it there is literally no Law. (There are exceptions. The Government has always controlled the roads and official buildings and a killing may be murder on a strip of concrete where a half a dozen feet away it is the exclusive concern of *Pukhtunwali*.) The visitor, when he enters tribal territory, depends for his safety on the protection of the Pakistani Government (one does not harm the ward of a powerful and friendly neighbour) and upon *Pukhtunwali*. These two things, it must be proclaimed to the credit of everyone concerned, make for more personal security than is to be had in many a sophisticated metropolis of the West.

The Pathans have been little subjected to the spirit-chilling devices of modern anthropology. Few of them have ever been forced to puzzle over one of Rorschach's blobs. I know of no scholar who can claim to have counted the number of times an Afridi housewife carries water from the well each day. Yet there is much knowledge to be gained from contact and friendship with the people and from study of their history and literature.

Their way of life includes many things, some valued and some scorned in the West. *Melmastia*, it must be confessed, is more a matter of personal prestige and self-aggrandisement than of charity or brotherly love. *Badal* springs from pride and retribution rather than from a desire to promote the common good or the rehabilitation of the offender. Yet the least which can be said is that the Pathans are a strong and free people in a time when it is not easy for those possessed of neither nuclear weapons nor massive sums of money to be either.

As for the 'character' of the Pathans, one of their own favourite folk-tales portrays it graphically. In summary form, the story runs like this:

'Once a great prince had a very beautiful wife. Her greatest charm was her eyes, which mirrored all the wonderful things she saw or thought about.

'One day the prince, who was very much in love with her, noticed a dullness in her eyes. Despite all the doctors could do the dullness increased day by day. The prince called all his coun- sellors together and asked them what to do.

'Omar the Poet recommended that the prince be grateful for all the beauty that he had enjoyed in the eyes of his princess and that he accept the affliction, making it easier by taking the colour of his own dreams and the light from his own heart and pouring them into the eyes of his wife. "Then," said Omar, "you will remember and see again the beauty that once came forth from the eyes of your princess."

' "Slop and nonsense! Fiddlesticks and make-believe!" said Khalil the Wise. "Be wise and practical, my prince. The World is full of beautiful girls with shining eyes. I will bring you a bevy from the Valley of Shameem who will turn your house into a firefly garden on a summer night!"

'The grieving prince was furious. He pulled out Khalil's beard and sent him away.

'Rahman the Seer spoke next. "In the mountains beyond the river lives a man whom the World calls a beggar. But he has in his heart a pool of something that will cure any ailment, for it has conquered time and death. Go find him, my prince. Ask for the magic liquid and put a drop in each eye of your princess. They will shine lovelier, brighter and dreamier than before."

'The prince was glad and set out with all his followers to find the beggar.

'Eventually he did and he asked him, "What have you in your heart?"

' "Love and laughter," replied the beggar.

' "Will you give me two drops of it for my wife?"

' "Yes, if you will pay the price."

' "Name it," said the prince.

' "Your kingdom for the drop of laughter, and your pride for the drop of love," answered the beggar.

' "Too high! My kingdom and my power have been given me by Allah. Since you are so unloving of your prince, I deem you unfit to hold your treasure and confiscate it in the name of the Law and of the people."

'The prince had the beggar put in chains and took him home and cast him into prison.

'The next morning, when the door of the prison was opened, behold, by the grace of Allah, nothing was there but a heap of rags, skin and bone. The beggar had gone and taken his love and laughter with him.

'When the prince saw this he was very angry, because he had never been defeated before.

'He was very angry with all his counsellors and pulled out all their beards.

'He was very angry with the princess because it was for her sake that he had been defeated, and he said, "Damn her eyes!"

'Then he sent for Khalil the Wise and went with him to the Valley of Shameem with fine horses, musicians, hawks and greyhounds, and forgot his one defeat in many blissful conquests.

'But the poor little princess . . .

'She is nearly blind.'

VI

Guardians of the Passes

IN MARCH 1947 a party of Afridi *maliks* called on Sir Olaf
Caroe at Government House in Peshawar. Sir Olaf, the British
Governor of the North-West Frontier, was a man in a difficult
position. London had decided a few months earlier that India was
to be given its freedom. The predominantly Hindu Congress
Party was seeking to preserve a united independent India. The
Muslim League was fighting desperately for a separate Pakistan.
The Afridis, about 275,000 of whom live in and around the
Khyber Pass, had already cut the pass three times since the begin-
ning of the year.

His callers did little to lighten Sir Olaf's burdens. They had
come to discuss the political situation, they said, and announced
(according to the *New York Times*): 'We won't deal with a
Congress Party. We won't deal with the Muslim League. We
may deal with a government representing both sides. We own
the Khyber Pass and will bargain on that basis.'

In hectoring Sir Olaf, the Afridis were acting in accordance
with a venerated tradition. Soon after the British took over the
Frontier in 1849 they had been faced with the necessity of securing
the passes. Inevitably they found themselves dealing with the
Afridis.

The new conquerors took a leaf from the book of the Moguls
who had preceded them by four hundred years. They offered the
Afridis allowances for protecting, that is, not attacking, traffic
through the strategic Kohat Pass, which connected Peshawar with
Kohat to the south, and through the Khyber, which led westwards into Afghanistan.

They promised the Adam Khel Afridis who lived in the Kohat
Pass an annual allowance of 5,700 rupees for good behaviour.
Long before the first year's allowance had been earned the Adam
Khel reverted to its old custom of ambushing and looting cara-
vans. Sir Charles Napier, commander-in-chief of all the British

forces in India, and more than 3,000 soldiers came up to the Frontier to stop this.

The Adam Khel gave over its bad habits while the soldiers were present. As soon as they left, raiding commenced again. This time the British were more subtle. They offered the Orakzais, who lived nearby, 8,000 rupees to protect the pass. This worked for a few weeks, but then the fighting between the Adam Khel and the Orakzais became so intense that the pass was unsafe once more. At this point, a third subsidy for protection of the pass was given to the Bangash. The three-way tribal feud which resulted drew the fighting well away from the pass.

The Kuki Khel Afridis who lived near the entrance to the Khyber Pass at Fort Jamrud presented a more difficult problem. They were happy to forfeit the subsidy which had been promised them in favour of the richer pickings to be had from the increased caravan trade to and from Peshawar. Their fellow clans were not prepared to go to war with the powerful Kuki Khel. None of the tribesmen could be easily got at in the mountain fastnesses which bordered the Khyber and it was virtually impossible to locate and arrest an individual offender.

To meet the problem Sir Herbert Edwardes (his name is perpetuated in Edwardes College in Peshawar) devised a new technique, that of collective responsibility. This meant that the whole khel or tribe would be held responsible for the wrong-doings of any of its members. Edwardes' first attempt to apply his theory was notably successful and collective responsibility remained one of the major British methods of administration until 1947.

In 1853 a British messenger was waylaid in the Khyber and several bottles of quinine (which the Pathans still consider the only medicine worthy of their note) were taken from him. The Kuki Khel Afridis denied all knowledge of the robbery. Edwardes thereupon ordered every Kuki Khel found in Peshawar to be imprisoned. As an incentive, he offered a reward of thirty rupees for each tribesman turned over to him.

So well did the other tribes respond that by nightfall of the first day, several hundred rupees' worth of Kuki Khel reposed in the Peshawar jail. The Kuki Khel elders returned the quinine the next morning. Edwardes, acutely conscious of the Government's limited finances, made them reimburse him for the rewards he had paid before opening the jail doors.

Of the Afridi *khels*, the most notorious is the Zakka Khel. Throughout their history they have made a fetish out of brigandage. So well have they succeeded that the other *khels* refuse to accept the word of a Zakka Khel, but insist that he swear upon the Holy Koran before believing him.

In 1888 Kipling took note of the reputation of the Zakka Khel in his 'Lament of the Border Cattle Thief', and, indeed, there are few words which better express the spirit of the Zakka Khel:

> They have taken away my long jezail,
> My shield and sabre fine,
> And heaved me into the Central Jail
> For lifting of the kine . . .
>
> But for the sorrow and the shame,
> The brand on me and mine,
> I'll pay you back in leaping flame
> And loss of the butchered kine.
>
> For every cow I spared before
> In charity set free,
> If I may reach my hold once more
> I'll reive an honest three . . .
>
> 'Tis war, red war, I'll give you then,
> War till my sinews fail;
> For the wrong you have done to a chief of men,
> And a thief of the Zukka Kheyl.

Sure enough red war came in the two decades which followed. The Zakka Khel perfected their craft in the Nineties, stealing from the rich Hindu merchants of the plains, sheltering and assisting lesser bands of thieves from Afghanistan and other parts of the Frontier. In 1904 they went down into Kohat and robbed and murdered a wealthy merchant. Wearing stolen constabulary uniforms they penetrated into Peshawar itself in 1908 and relieved a Hindu banker of 100,000 rupees. On another occasion they attempted a train robbery and the kidnapping of a British assistant commissioner.

The Afridis of today are tall, handsome men; they possess a

calm and dignity that is remarkable even among Pathans. Blue
eyes and fair skin are not uncommon. The cloths they wind
around their *kullahs* (a dome-like basket which serves as the base
of a Pathan turban) are usually cleaner and their dress less ragged
than many of their brother tribes. They seem to have a particular
talent with mechanical contraptions and many of them have
prospered through operation of the score of bus lines which haul
phenomenal loads of freight and passengers through the passes.
Others appear as drivers and mechanics all over Pakistan, playing
much the same rôle as the Sikhs do in India. An Afridi bus driver
of today receives the few rupees fare from Peshawar to Kohat
with all the satisfaction and self-assurance with which his fore-
fathers took their toll in bales of Bokhara silk from cowering
caravanmen.

As far as I could ever determine, the Afridis are as orthodox
and devout Muslims as any other Pathans. Yet their reputation
for impiety goes far back. Khushal Khan Khattak, the Pathan
warrior-poet who was writing in the seventeenth century, mentions it several times. One of Khushal Khan's verses begins:

> My carnal heart is an Afridi, who cares nothing for
> religion;
> Its good thoughts are few, and it is very much given
> to wickedness.

The opening lines of another poem are:

> The call of the *muezzin* is not to be heard anywhere
> in the Afridi land,
> Unless you listen to the crowing of the cock at the
> dawn of the day.

One day while sitting in an Afridi *hujra* near the Khyber, I recalled Khushal Khan's words to some of my hosts.

"People have always said bad things about us," a *malik* agreed.
"Once, many generations ago, a *pir*, a very holy man, came to
visit us from Hind. He preached to our fathers of their sins and
upbraided them. He pointed out that in all of our country we did
not have a single tomb of a saint at which we might make our
devotions."

"So, it is true?" I said.

"Oh, no!" he replied. "Our fathers were much impressed with the *pir*'s words. So they killed him, and ever since his tomb has been a noble shrine."

When I returned to Peshawar I gleefully recounted this nugget of local lore to a sophisticated Pathan friend. "That story again!" he said. "Some Britisher who fancied himself a wit made it up twenty years ago. Those old fellows out at Jamrud tell it to amuse the tourists. You can find it in one of the books at the Club." I did find it in a badly written personal adventure published in the 1930s. My nugget lost much of its glitter.

A good many months later, going through the records in the India Office Library in London, I found the tale again. This time it was on the age-yellowed page of an official report written by a British official in the 1850s. He reported the story as being current among the Afridis and the Yusufzai of his time and accepted as true by both. It all goes to prove that one never can be sure about Afridis.

The same is true in many ways of their far-famed pass, the Khyber. Taken cold-bloodedly (I have met few men who could), the Khyber can be disappointing. The entrance is a scant dozen miles from Peshawar over a hard-surfaced, virtually level road. The pass itself is a passage through the hills rather than a high divide like those which nick the crests of the Himalayas and Karakorams. Its thirty-mile length lies entirely within Pakistan and one can drive through it in less than an hour. It is a mere 1,404 feet high at its end on the Afghan border, 1,670 feet at its entrance, and only 3,373 feet at its summit. Today, at least, it radiates peace and security.

But, however unimaginative or ill-informed the traveller may be, he has only to look a little more closely to sense the things which have struck a thrill into countless generations of men from all over the World. At the entrance to the pass on the edge of the Peshawar Plain stands Fort Jamrud, built by the Sikhs and in outline strongly resembling a battleship of First World War vintage. Here in a desperate battle in 1835 the great Sikh general Hari Singh was killed by the tribesmen.

At the other end, overlooking Afghanistan, is Torkhum, the check point on the international border. The Pakistani border officials there usually seem more interested in pressing tea and cakes on the travelling stranger than in going over his papers. The company at the Torkhum tea table is cosmopolitan. On one visit I shared Pathan hospitality with Mrs Eleanor Roosevelt; on another, with a party of smiling Russians wearing the high fur caps of Central Asia who were headed for Lahore on unknown business. A third time the tea table was crowded with a touring company of Chinese Communist 'artistes', three ambassadors *en route* to Kabul, a Dublin journalist on a walking tour of Asia, and a dapper pawnbroker of Australian nationality on his way to visit the village of his birth near Jelalabad.

In between Jamrud and Torkhum there is constant activity. Caravans plod along the twisting trail beside the double-lane cement road. Road signs bear neat pictures of motor-cars and camels, with arrows indicating the appropriate routes for each. In the autumn hordes of *powendas*, nomad Ghilzai Pathans, pour down from the Afghan highlands to winter in Pakistan, and overflow from the caravan trail on to the cement road. No one seems to mind.

Near Shagai Fort the rock-cliffs by the side of the road are emblazoned with the carved and painted crests of the British regiments who served in the pass. Above, cutting through the cliffs in a virtually continuous tunnel, runs the narrow gauge railway which the regiments guarded. Once a strategic lifeline, the railway now carries only one train a week; this is usually jammed with Pakistani tourists in holiday mood and there is no better way to see the Khyber than from the cab of its little engine.

The bustling bazaar at Landikotal, more than half-way through the pass, is always thronged with Afridis and Shinwaris; it surrounds the famous Khyber Rifles Mess, still full of gleaming silver and polished mahogany, which the Pakistani officers take care of as tenderly as did their British predecessors. Not far from Landikotal an enormous Buddhist *stupa* towers above the road, its contents long since looted, but its fifteen-hundred-year-old silhouette still a landmark for miles around.

It is an exciting experience to go up through the Khyber and from a knoll above Torkhum to look out upon the wastes of Afghanistan and imagine the great stretches of Central Asia which lie beyond. To be seen at its most formidable, however, the Khyber should be viewed coming down from Torkhum to Fort Jamrud, not going up. This is the way the great invaders saw it as they came down from the Central Asian plateau to reap the rich spoils of India. Redoubts of every description perch on the hilltops, their buttresses running down the slopes. A two-thousand-year-old wall protects a recently erected pillbox. A line of Second World War tank traps (put down at the time of the battle for Stalingrad, when the threat of a German invasion of South Asia from the Caucasus was a reality) is anchored to an ancient battlement of dressed, unmortared stone.

There is not a yard of the road which is not commanded by three or four fortifications. Most of them are abandoned now, but their empty gunports still peer down on the traveller below. It is not difficult to imagine ghosts of the past flitting along the crumbling battlements and seeking shelter in deserted pickets on the hilltops.

History hangs heavy on the Khyber and has left its mark upon its sombre stone. Ground into the dust of the pass is Persian gold, Greek iron, Tatar leather, Mogul gems, Afghan silver and British steel. All have watered it with their blood. It is at once a relief and an anti-climax to reach Jamrud and look out over the villages of the plain to Peshawar.

The traditional heart of the Afridi homeland is the Tirah, a series of small valleys just south of the Khyber Pass, not more than thirty miles from Peshawar. The beauty and fertility of the Tirah is legendary among the Pathans. The peaks which surround its valleys can be seen from Peshawar University. There may be a few Englishmen still alive who can give a fuller description, but I cannot. British expeditionary forces fought their way into the area in 1898 and 1908. Since that time, few outsiders have penetrated into the Afridi's *sanctum sanctorum*.

The Afridis' 'other' pass (other than the Khyber, that is) is the most spectacular geographically of all the Frontier passes. Known simply as Darra, 'the Pass', to the tribesmen, but usually called the Kohat Pass in English, it cuts across the rim of the Peshawar Valley to connect the Frontier capital with the important cantonment town of Kohat.

The road zigzags up the side of the hills with almost unbelievable steepness. Modern motor vehicles do not find the climb easy and when one vehicle stalls, traffic waits behind it. Here and there the shattered bodies of trucks dot the slopes below the road. These grim reminders have no appreciable effect on the grinning Afridi drivers who spin their vehicles around the hairpin turns at full speed.

At the top of the pass is the Handyside Gate, named after a famous British police officer. From the Gate one has a panoramic view of Kohat and the surrounding plain below. On the way down, villages nestle in fertile little side valleys, and along the main road are the Afridi gun factories.

These gun factories are a major industry on the Frontier. Others dot the Afridi country, but those in the Darra and at Jamrud Village at the entrance to the Khyber are the largest and most readily accessible. Their chief products are excellent copies of the ·303 Enfield rifle, the ·455 Webley revolver, and the Sten gun. Practically all of the gun-making equipment is hand-operated and days are spent rifling a barrel. To increase customers' trust, the weapons are stamped with traditional British markings. The dies for the markings have been carefully counterfeited, but they are not always applied with consistency. (I have seen a single Enfield stamped both Mark III and Mark IV.) As a result, gun fanciers in far parts of the World who occasionally come into possession of an Afridi-made weapon sometimes find themselves puzzling over the apparent madness of Her Britannic Majesty's ordnance.

The local rifles sell for two or three hundred rupees (£15–£23). The sum represents more than a year's cash earnings to most tribesmen, but is far less than the three to five thousand rupees which an authentic British-made Enfield would fetch in the tribal area. The Afridi rifles are well made and accurate, though both barrel rifling and bolt tend to erode badly after a few hundred rounds have been fired.

In British days the Afridis preferred stealing the bolts to making them. Many a Tommy who went to sleep with his rifle securely tucked between his legs woke up to find the bolt missing and to thank God that he himself was intact. According to local lore, the degree of skill which the Afridis developed in bolt-snatching eventually caused the British command to issue standing orders that all bolts were to be removed from army rifles at night and locked in a steel chest in the custody of the sergeant-major. When an Afridi mentions this bit of information to you the chances are that he is working up to a story about how his father stole the chest.

(*Above*) Gunsmith in the Darra between Peshawar and Kohat

(*Right*) *Khassadar* (levy) in the south of Waziristan

(*Above*) Tribal school near the Darra

(*Left*) An Afridi *malik*

· The Afridis sell their handicraft to all comers, and the gun factory at Darra is as cosmopolitan a place as the mosque of Mahabat Khan in Peshawar. Wazirs, Mahsuds and Mohmands make a week's journey on foot in order to look over the stock. Many will stay for a few days to select their weapon, a choice which they consider one of the most important of their lives. No one knows exactly how many weapons the Afridis have produced for the tribes, but there is no doubt that they have made a major contribution to the more than half a million rifles which are now estimated to be in private hands in the tribal area.

Rifles, Afridis and the Darra figured prominently in the Ellis Case, one of the most famous incidents to take place on the Frontier in British days. The personalities and incidents involved in the Ellis Case are still well known locally today.

It all began in February 1923 when a number of rifles were stolen from the British cantonment at Kohat. Intense police work by Mr Handyside laid the theft at the door of one Ajab Khan, a Bosti Khel Afridi whose village lay in the Darra. Handyside led a combined force of police and regular-army soldiers in a search of Ajab's village, which resulted in the recovery of some of the missing rifles and a good deal of other stolen property. Ajab himself was away at the time of the raid.

According to the official record, the operation was conducted 'with all possible regard for tribal susceptibilities', but the story got around—and persists today—that some of the village women were subjected to search and insult.

Goaded on by his women and relatives, Ajab planned his *badal*. In April he raided Kohat again, creeping into the heart of the cantonment under cover of darkness with several accomplices. In the course of the raid the wife of a British officer, Mrs Ellis, was killed, and her daughter, Mollie, a girl of about fifteen, carried off.

This profanation of British womanhood caused violent emotions in the hearts of most Britons in India and at home and there was much talk of mass reprisal against the Afridis. Eventually, however, the girl was returned unharmed as the result of a series of complicated negotiations carried on mainly by two Pathan political officers, Khan Bahadur Mogul Beg Khan and Khan Bahadur Kuli Khan.

Then the hunt for Ajab Khan and his associates in crime began in earnest. The British threatened blockade and suspension of allowances for any tribe which gave refuge to the fugitives. Ajab crossed in and out of Afghanistan several times and finally turned himself over to the Afghan governor of Jelalabad in 1924. He and his family, which had managed to join him, were taken to Kabul, despite British demands for their surrender, and there was some talk by British officers in Peshawar of going to get Ajab without recourse to international procedures.

Even if the Kabul Government had wanted to, widespread hatred of the British in Afghanistan would have prevented the return of the fugitives. At last the Government let it become known that Ajab and his family were being 'interned' beyond the Hindu Kush, far from the Indian Frontier, and he was given land near Mazaar-i-Sharif.

His accomplices fared less well. They returned secretly across the border to live in the Tirah. Eventually the most notorious of them, Gul Akhbar, was caught and hanged in Peshawar, in 1928.

Ajab's clan, the Bosti Khel Afridis, was fined 42,000 rupees in cash and rifles as a result of the incident, and Ajab's personal lands were confiscated. His village was demolished and, according to local legend, the site was ploughed with salt. The tribes which had harboured him during his flight were fined 20,000 rupees.

All of this was more than thirty years ago. Ajab lived on in northern Afghanistan, aged and respectable, until his death a year or two ago. In late 1952 Ajab's brother, Shahzada, returned for the first time to the site of his ancestral village for what he described as a brief 'sentimental journey'. I happened to be in the neighbourhood, and watched as his clansmen garlanded him with flowers and the local Pakistani government officials (the British were now five years gone) came to shake his hand.

The journey turned out to be something more than purely sentimental. A few months after returning to Afghanistan, Shahzada led a *lashkar* of Pathans hostile to Pakistan back across the border to promote the 'Pushtoonistan' movement which, with Afghan support, promotes the cause of an independent state for the Pathans of Pakistan.

In 1954, while on a visit to Afghanistan, I met Shahzada again in Kabul. Over a cup of tea I reminded him of his 'sentimental journey' and asked him if there had been any connection between his two visits to Pakistan. Eyes twinkling, he replied with the Pushtu equivalent of 'no comment'.

The British used to say that a dozen years of peace on the Frontier was inevitably a prelude to war. Their theory was simple and sound. During the years of peace boys grew into young men without tasting battle. Soon they could no longer stand having to remain silent in the *hujras* when their elders recounted great deeds. Then, they went out to perform some of their own.

The departure of the British has made it more difficult for young hotheads to find a means of proving their valour. Yet they can still do so when the occasion demands.

A few years ago a young Afridi tribesman who lived in a village near the Khyber contracted for a marriage with a girl from Peshawar. It is the custom of the hill tribesmen to 'buy' their brides by payment of a sum of money to the girl's family. In this case the money had been accepted but the girl's family delayed sending her to the prospective husband, pleading that her mother needed her and that she was not yet old enough to stand the harsher life of the hills.

The young Afridi put up with this for a few months and then decided on direct action. He could not readily get at the girl or her family in the security of the city. So he went down to the grounds of Islamia College near the university one night and kidnapped the first student he came upon. The fact that the student had no connection with the girl or her family and that he did not even know about the injustice which they had perpetrated made no difference to the tribesman. The boy was one of the people of the plains who had betrayed him. That was enough. With his hostage in his hands, the Afridi sent down word to the authorities that he would trade the student for his wife.

The political agent went out to negotiate. Being an official he could not approve of kidnapping, nor could he force an unwilling woman to leave her family. And yet, being a Pathan himself, he could not help but understand the basic righteousness of the tribesman's position. After much negotiation the student was set free and the marriage money, but not the girl, returned to the frustrated bridegroom. According to one rumour, a rifle and a few cartridges were added to sweeten the bargain. In such a manner even today is honour appeased and peace maintained among the Afridis.

VII

Beyond the Malakand

I FIRST DROVE UP through the Malakand Pass with a Pushtu-speaking driver whose command of my language was as limited as mine of his. He had been instructed by the officials in Peshawar who arranged the trip to point out the sights, and he did so enthusiastically. We inspected the headworks of the Upper Swat Canal. We poked about in mounds at the side of the road which could have covered Alexander's campsites. We turned aside to climb a ruined Buddhist *stupa*.

Tracing our route on a map, I had no trouble following the driver's enumeration of placenames until we passed one undistinguished hill at which he pointed and said something that sounded like 'Church Hill'. There was no sign of a structure, Muslim, Christian, or any other. The map made no mention of the place, and it was not until we got back to Peshawar that I discovered that this was the spot where Sir Winston Churchill, then a young subaltern, had received his baptism of fire and collected the material for his first book while serving with the Malakand Field Force more than half a century ago.

The Malakand Pass is a sparkling contrast to the sombre Khyber. Pine forests cover the flanks of the mountains. The cold blue waters of the Swat River tumble along below the road. The pass connects the three princely states of Swat, Dir and Chitral with the rest of Pakistan, but it is less a passage between two places than a step up the long ascent which leads through high green valleys to the mightiest mountain massif on earth. At the end of the valleys, rank on rank, the great mountain tiers rise, leaving the impression that there can be no way through them, and nothing beyond them.

The entrance to Swat State, a picture-book fort with four square towers, stands beside the rushing waters of the river. We stopped for tea in the police station placed in the base of one of the towers. An elderly sub-inspector with waxed handle-bar

66

moustache worthy of a British sergeant-major presided over the tea-pot. The few hundred words of English he had at his disposal, as well as his hearty, no-nonsense manner and bulging muscles, would also have become his British counterpart.

He pointed at an antique telephone hanging on the wall. "With those, our Miangul conquered this state," he announced. "He built forts like this everywhere. He put telephones in them. Every time those beggars in the hills made trouble, we would call him up and tell him. Then he would send more men or come himself. We tell his son, the Wali Sahib, who is now our king, everything too. You watch."

He marched over, cranked the instrument, and shouted into it. "Now they expect you in Saidu," he said. "When you get to our capital, all will be in readiness. If you do not go straight there, everybody will know too," he added. The last remark, I gathered, was meant to encourage us to stay on the road and not to go wandering off into the hills where we might cause trouble and necessitate another call to the Wali.

Stirring things have happened in the hills which surround the Swat Valley. A few miles north and west of Chakdarra is a great pile of ruins which Sir Olaf Caroe deems to be the site of Alexander's battle of Massaga mentioned by the historians Arrian and Curtius. Off to the east, above the Indus, is the Pir Sar Ridge, which Sir Aurel Stein has identified as the Rock of Aornos, site of another of the Macedonian's battles.

Sixty years ago, during the great tribal rising of 1897, the Mulla Mastun (known to the British as 'the Mad Mulla') proclaimed a holy war against the British from his village nearby. He took with him a few boys from his mosque school, proclaimed one of them king of Delhi, and marched off on *jihad*. Within three days he had gathered 20,000 tribesmen from the surrounding hills and attacked the British posts at Chakdarra and in the Malakand Pass. After a week of fighting 'the Mad Mulla' and his warriors disappeared as quickly and as strangely as they had come, leaving behind them several hundred of their own and British dead.

For the next few decades virtual anarchy reigned in the valley as various local chieftains fought each other. The British chose to ignore the situation as long as the competitors did not come into conflict with the interests of the central government. Finally one of the petty chieftains from the relatively unimportant Safi tribe of Pathans succeeded in founding the present state of Swat. This was the Miangul, the present ruler's father.

The Miangul, in addition to being a first-class warrior, was the grandson of the Akhund of Swat, a religious leader who figured prominently among the local tribes in the nineteenth century. He made use both of the saintly reputation of his family and his own remarkable talent for organisation to carve out the Swat State. He constructed forts at strategic points throughout the valley, installed telephones in them, and left small permanent garrisons. The old-fashioned *lashkar* tactics used by his opponents were no match for the Miangul's modern approach, and in a short time he had won British recognition for his state. Shortly before the British left India the Miangul retired and turned the state over to his son, Jehanzeb.

Jehanzeb has also produced some surprises. We knew that there was a hotel in Saidu, the capital of Swat, which lies half-way up the valley. The Wali had built it recently because the growing number of visitors to his state had threatened to crowd him out of his modest palace, which in the past had also served as an official guest-house.

We had not known that the hotel would be a pure delight, combining Pathan charm with European convenience. There was no doubt that my wife and I were expected. A fire crackled in the room into which we were led. In front of it a massive silver tea service glistened, its shadow dancing on the whitewashed walls. These were hung with brightly-coloured 'Swat blankets', roughly woven tapestries akin to those of the Navajos in the American South-West. A broad window provided a vista for miles up the valley to the chain of saw-tooth mountains which shut out Soviet Central Asia beyond. A few stars twinkling above snow-mantled peaks completed the Christmas-card scenery.

The bathroom sparkled with porcelain and chromium. The tap marked 'hot' poured out steaming water when turned. "I'm glad you warned me we would have to rough it out here in tribal territory," Edith remarked as she took advantage of the full-length mirror in the bathroom door. (We had never been able to find such a mirror in Karachi for our own house and two attempts to have one imported had added up to fourteen years' bad luck.)

The next morning an aide-de-camp to the Wali brought word that we were expected to inspect the school. The ruler, he explained suavely, was busy—'on a matter of state'. His highness hoped to see us later. Meanwhile we were free to go anywhere we wanted in the valley.

The paint was still wet on the newly plastered walls of the school. It was, the principal told us, now being used as a high school. The following year, those who were capable of further study would continue in college classes which were being set up. After that, the college would be the top of an academic pyramid based on a school in each village of the state.

I thought I had caught evidence of Asia's great educational fallacy: beginning at the top. "And when will the village schools be set up?" I asked slyly. "Our Wali has been working on that. Since last year each village has at least one. Saidu has several," I was told.

A blackboard covered one wall of the veranda. A young man with a squawking radio beside him was writing the news of the day in chalk. Intermingled with the flowing Arabic script were English words: 'President Eisenhower', 'Senator McCarthy', 'Malenkov'. Swat, we reflected, was not so far out of the World as one might think.

Our educational visitation was brief. The deep green valley and the white-capped mountains beyond were too much of a temptation. We set off up the valley towards Kalam, the road head from which caravans of shaggy camels take off to cross 16,000-foot passes between 25,000-foot peaks.

Our passage through wayside villages produced a remarkable effect. Soldiers and policemen dashed from tea-houses to present arms. Troops of children appeared waving flags and singing. In almost every village a group of elders looked after us in amazement and concern as our green Chevrolet station-wagon passed on without stopping.

"What's going on?" I asked the driver. This time language was no barrier. He shrugged his shoulders, as bewildered as we were.

A dozen miles below Kalam a cloud of dust appeared on the road ahead of us. Vehicles are few in Swat and the road was narrow at this point, so we pulled off to let whatever was coming go by. A green Chevrolet station-wagon slammed to a halt beside us. It was identical to ours in every respect save one: it was flying the royal flag. A dozen (Edith counted them surreptitiously, I discovered later) armed men poured out. In their midst, distinguished only by a clean-shaven face and a shirt somewhat newer than the rest, was the Wali of Swat.

As we climbed out to meet him, one word of English came to our driver. "The King," he announced, grinning broadly.

After an orgy of handshaking the Wali took command. "My apologies, Sir, Madam," he said. "I am sorry that you will not be able to go all the way to Kalam. A bridge fell last night between here and there. I have been trying to fix it but it will not be finished until tomorrow."

This, I decided, was the 'matter of state' of which the Wali's aide had spoken.

The Wali was eager to get on to other matters. He invited us to breakfast the following morning: "My house . . . will 6 a.m. be all right?" Then he jumped behind the wheel of his station-wagon again; his escort jumped in with him, and the vehicle continued down the road at a break-neck speed.

Smiling villagers and shouting children greeted us on the way back to Saidu, but our royal reception was not repeated. They knew now that there could be two green Chevrolet station-wagons in so great a kingdom as theirs.

Six o'clock seemed a bit early for breakfast, even with a king, but we left a call at the hotel for five-thirty. The room servant did not understand at first, but was delighted to learn that 'five-thirty' means to an American what 'half-five' does to an Englishman. He went off muttering his new phrase to himself.

Bed tea arrived at 5.10 a.m., for in Pakistan a traveller never need fear being called late. Rising to pray at dawn, the Muslims make the most of the early morning. In Swat the early hours have nothing in common with the cold grey dawn of Europe and America, and there is a sparkling charm about them which inspires even the most lethargic body to take on new life.

The Wali's 'palace' is a handsome, unpretentious building on a slight rise above Saidu. Our host and an aide met us on the steps, for Pathan hospitality is gracious as well as bountiful. Inside, a fire had been laid in an enormous fireplace. On the opposite side of the room a great window gave out on the same, almost unbelievable view across the roofs of the town, over the villages of the valley clothed in the haze of the morning cooking fires, and to the splendid bulwark of the mountains.

Jehanzeb the Wali radiated charm and vigour. He was brought up in Swat and educated in Islamia College at Peshawar; he now rules firmly and benevolently over his kingdom. By 'matters of state' was meant schools, roads and irrigation canals. By 7 a.m. the telephone was jingling constantly and a secretary was laying out piles of correspondence at the Wali's elbow. When we took our leave he accompanied us to the car and spoke a few words of Pushtu to the driver, who grinned and shook the Wali's hand. "*Pa mukha dai khuh!*" (May goodness go before you!) said the ruler as he sent us off.

Swat is a model of progress and stability to the neighbouring states of Dir and Chitral. Dir remains in a remarkable state of backwardness, and her ruler, the Nawab, refused even to send representatives to the West Pakistan legislative assembly in 1956. (He has since been deposed by the Government of Pakistan and the heir-apparent, Prince Khusro, installed in his place.)

Chitral is noted chiefly as the birthplace of polo and for its bloody dynastic struggles, the most formidable of which took place in 1892 after the death of the 'Great Mehtar', Aman-ul-Mulk. Within a year sixteen of Aman-ul-Mulk's seventeen sons were disposed of violently in the struggle for succession. The problem was solved only when the British moved in and installed on the throne the surviving son, Shuja-ul-Mulk, described by a contemporary British writer as 'an intelligent, trustworthy, little boy, nine or ten years old'.

In Chitral and much of the northern parts of Dir and Swat live a people whom the Pathans call Kohistanis, the 'people of the mountains'. They are of diverse racial origins—Mongol, Chinese, Tatar, Iranian and original Aryan—and speak dozens of different languages and dialects. The legend persists among some of them that they are the descendants of Alexander's Greeks. Many are Shiite Muslims, owing spiritual allegiance to the Aga Khan and his local lieutenant, the Mir of Hunza, the ruler of a tiny state high in the mountains of Gilgit.

There is only one spot in all this vast area which Islam has failed to encompass. In three little valleys, just north of the Lawari Pass which connects Dir and Chitral, live the Kafirs, light-skinned, fair-haired people who still hold to their own uninhibited form of paganism. There are only a few thousand Kafirs left and their way of life is primitive. However, the beauty and passion of the Kafir women is legendary throughout the Pathan country, and the fabled 'Valley of Shameem', to which the prince retired to forget himself in pleasure, probably lay in Kafiristan.

Wherever the Pathans live they are dominant. They expanded from their homeland in the Suleiman Hills southward until stopped by the deserts of Baluchistan. They pushed eastward to the barrier of the Indus, westward to the Hazarajat of Afghanistan. Why then, historians have long wondered, did they not spread all the way up the northern valleys to the main wall of the Pamirs?

An answer to this question thoroughly consistent with Pathan character emerged just a few years ago. Frederick Barth, a Norwegian anthropologist who did considerable work in Swat, discovered that the line between Pathans and Kohistanis coincided almost exactly with that where double-cropping ceased to be possible. Over the centuries, the Pathan invaders had driven the Kohistanis northward to this point. When it was reached, the pressure stopped.

Why did it stop? Because the invaders had reached the limit of the area which could support the 'way of the Pathan', which involves the pursuit of honour, leisure and war as well as agriculture. The higher region, where a man may, on a single crop and some herding, merely exist, was left to the Kohistanis.

VIII

The Sons of Joseph

IN DECEMBER 1956 the Chinese Communist premier Chou En-lai visited Pakistan. He got a cool reception. However, Pakistan has a common border with the powerful Communist state, and Chou's hosts did not want him to return home feeling entirely unappreciated. Someone had the bright idea of making him a blood-brother of the Yusufzai.

A few Yusufzai khans were found who were willing to go along with the idea, and, in due course, Chou was accepted into the clan. A photograph showing him wearing a turban and an uneasy smile was published around the World. As one cynical newspaperman pointed out, the whole thing was most appropriate; the Communist leader's name is pronounced 'Joe', and the Yusufzai are the sons of Yusuf, or Joseph.

While the idea of blood brotherhood is known among the Pathans, it is not nearly so common as it was among the Indian tribes of the American West. It is usually reserved for the rare outsider who has established a close degree of intimacy and respect with the Pathans. In the 'Ballad of East and West' Kipling was paying the ultimate compliment to his young hero when he had him take "the Oath of the Brother-in-Blood on leavened bread and salt . . . on fire and fresh-cut sod, On the hilt and the haft of the Khyber knife and the Wondrous Names of God".

The chronicles of the Yusufzai are ancient, going back well beyond the days when the Pathan genealogies were created by the Mogul historians. So pure have the Yusufzai kept their blood-lines and so rigorously have they obeyed the Pathan code that they are universally acknowledged by the other tribes as being the most blue-blooded Pathans of all. This is a rare compliment, since most Pathans spend a great deal of time impugning the Pathan-ness of other Pathans.

Needless to say, therefore, most Yusufzai were anything but happy over their newly-created kinship with the proletarian

Chinese. Equally inevitably, the other tribes enjoyed the rare joke at the expense of the exclusive Yusufzai.

Most of the Pathans who live in Dir and Swat in tribal territory are Yusufzai. However, the clan is to be seen at its most formidable in Mardan District, a deceptively peaceful-looking land of lush fields of wheat, corn, sugar-cane and tobacco. Here the settled Yusufzai inhabit a broad belt running from the banks of the Indus River to the Malakand Pass. Traditionally most of them owe allegiance to one or other of the great Yusufzai khans whose seats are at Mardan, Hoti, Zaida, Toru, Topi, and at half a dozen other ancient villages. These khans have in the past been the largest land-owners on the Frontier, some of them holding more than 20,000 acres.

Since the departure of the British in 1947 these large land holdings have been under virtually continuous attack, first by Khan Abdul Qaiyum Khan, then chief minister of the Frontier Province, and more recently by the land reform programme of President Ayub. Even apart from modern efforts at land reform, however, the Pathans have always had a democratic system of land tenure, which has resulted in the existence of a large number of small freeholders.

This system, which probably had its highest degree of development among the Yusufzai, reflects the passionate devotion of the Pathans to the land. In fact, a Pathan's very 'citizenship' in the tribe rests on his right to a share, or daftar, in the land.

When the tribes moved on to their present holdings, each set aside about half of the land for common grazing. The remainder was shared out in roughly equal parts to each of the khels, or major clans, within the tribe. Each of these portions were then divided among the various families of the khel, with a smaller area being held in common. Of the latter, a portion was set aside for the support of the mosque and its Imam (priest). Then each householder got an equal allotment. This descended to the owner's sons in equal shares, as did the rights in the common land of both his particular khel and of the tribe.

The individual's assigned plot was called bukhra. His share in the common land was known as inam. Bukhra and inam together constituted his daftar, or share, and all real Pathans are daftaris. After several generations, when fragmentation became extreme, a jirga divided some of the common land and apportioned it into shares to supplement each man's *bukhra*. A man might sell his *bukhra* and retain his membership in the tribe by virtue of his *inam*. Alienation of the latter was possible but very rare, for it cost a man his place in the tribe.

For centuries the Pathans practised a custom reminiscent of the early tribes of Israel. This called for periodic exchange of land among individual members of a tribe and between entire clans and tribes. The idea, called *wesh*, was to allow every member of the group and each of the various groups to enjoy the best land for some time and thus to prevent the development of leadership based on economic power.

These exchanges persisted among the Yusufzai until the middle of the last century. They took place at varying intervals, five, ten, or thirty years, and, surprisingly, usually took place without bloodshed. In some of the more remote areas of Dir, Bajaur and Buner, the custom was still observed to take place in the 1930s. However, it has vanished now.

The history of the Yusufzai country has never been set down in a book. However, it can be read on the spot—or at least guessed at—by the most amateur archaeologist.

A dozen miles above Attock, on the west bank of the Indus, a crumbling village inhabited by a number of elderly Yusufzai brothers perches atop an enormous mound of shattered masonry. Today it is called the Hund Village. In the chronicles of ancient India it was called *Ohind*, the Gate to India.

Mahmud of Ghazni passed this way in 1001 on the first of his many invasions of India. The Hindu maharaja, Jaipal, whom Mahmud defeated, may have waited for him at this spot. Mahmud was not the first visitor. Beneath the rubble of Mogul bricks may be seen the massive walls of dressed unmortared stone which are the mark of the Buddhist civilisation of the time of Christ. Even earlier the Greeks, and possibly Alexander himself, crossed the Indus at this point. Their coins may still be picked up in the neighbouring fields.

Half a dozen miles away lies the village of Lahor, atop another mount rich in the remains of the past. In many cases it is probably this village, not the great city in the Punjab, which is the Lahore mentioned in the medieval histories of the Muslim conquerors.

A mile or two below Hund at Rana Deri are the summer homes of the khans of Zaida, an aristocratic Yusufzai family. The buildings, complete with their own mosque, sit on a grassy knoll high above the rushing waters. Formal gardens, complete with peacocks, stretch down to the riverbank. Inside the main house are striking pieces of Graeco-Buddhist sculpture, unearthed nearby, which humble the collection in New York's Metropolitan Museum and compare well with those in the British Museum. Sitting on the veranda, one commands a view for miles up and down the river and across it to the Punjab shore. On sandbars and islets in the river small groups of the local folk may be seen panning for the gold the river brings down from the high mountains. At the turn of the seasons flights of geese and duck pass overhead *en route* to and from the great Central Asian plateau.

It was while in pursuit of a shot at a few of these ducks that my wife and I had a very intimate introduction to the Indus one March afternoon.

Our host, one of the khans of Zaida, suggested casually after tea that we go across to an island and try our luck. He passed out a brace of shot-guns and we strolled down to the riverbank where four of his retainers got busy preparing boats.

Two came carrying *charpoys* ('four-legs'), the rough country beds made of rope stretched over a wooden frame. The other two began blowing up cattle hides which lay in a pile on the bank. Our boats were ready in less than five minutes. There were two, each consisting of a pair of inflated skins supporting a *charpoy*. Blankets were thrown across the open rope matting for seats. Rudders and motive power were added when the boys jumped into the water and stretched out behind the craft.

A heated discussion of the course to be followed in crossing the roaring river followed. The khan seemed to be disagreeing with the boatmen and they with each other. Finally, he motioned me on to one *charpoy* and Edith on to the other. We sat cross-legged as instructed. I expected him to join her, for he was a chivalrous man and had been extremely solicitous for her welfare throughout our visit. Besides, this would have made for a more equitable distribution of weight, roughly fourteen stone, eight and a half stone, and fourteen stone.

However, he leaped from the bank on to my *charpoy*, shouted an order, and in a moment both craft were caught by the swift current. We whirled downstream for a few hundred yards, our human outboard motors hanging on desperately to the back of the bed frames, apparently lifeless, their faces often submerged. Peering like an artist across his upraised thumb at some landmark on the bank, our captain suddenly shouted again. The swimmers came to life. Their legs churned and we struggled a dozen yards across the stream until we were caught by an eddy, and obliquely moving upstream, were carried out into the centre of the channel. Here our course was suddenly reversed again by the main rush of the river. Just as it appeared that we would end the excursion by being dashed against some vicious-looking rocks, there was another shout. More thrashing of legs followed and we began to move laboriously across the current.

An icy feeling settled upon my lower limbs as four inches of the Indus streamed across my seat and crossed legs. It moved up to my heart when I saw that the swimmers were not only thrashing their legs to move us but blowing frantically into the leaky skins to keep us afloat. Abruptly, we were caught up again by another current, and after ninety seconds of smooth swift movement more like a ski run than a boat ride, we skidded up on the sandy beach of the islet. The swimmers crawled out grinning. The khan and I scrambled erect, dripping from the waist down. The cattle skins with a final gentle *pouf* collapsed entirely.

Edith strolled up, calm and dry, cradling the shot-guns in her arms. "My, you two heavyweights certainly do ride low in the water," she said.

We did not get any ducks, but we did manage to get safely back across the river in the same precipitous manner.

The next day we had a demonstration of the democratic traditions of the Pathans. The khan greeted us early in the morning and led me aside, explaining that he had an apology to make. It appeared that he had neglected to introduce me to the old man who guarded the guest-house where we were staying and kept it supplied with hot water. The retainer had interpreted this as a slight, and in a stormy night session with his khan had made it clear that he would no longer serve a Yusufzai who had so departed from the traditions of his people.

Before anything else could be done that day, the khan explained, this affair had to be remedied. I was duly presented to the aggrieved Pathan. We shook hands solemnly and wished each other well. Trying to carry the matter off as well as possible, I formally expressed my gratitude for his care of us and placed our security in his hands. The old man was placated but got in a parting shot. "He knows our ways better than you, it seems, Master," he said to the khan.

I expected to find the khan amused at the incident, but he was not. "Dear me," he said later in his best Oxford accent, "I made a frightful blunder. I wonder that he ever forgave me." I took the lesson to heart, and ever since have grabbed the hand of everyone in sight when joining a group of Pathans. The vigour with which they inevitably reciprocate suggests that they approve.

In the afternoon the khan took me on a stroll through his fields and I got a glimpse of how the Pathans view the World. We stopped to talk to an old man working on a drainage ditch. I gathered from the rapid-fire Pushtu that he had eye trouble and the khan had arranged for him to go away for an operation. In the old man's last words about the journey I thought I caught the phrase, "down to Hindustan".

"You are sending him to India?" I asked, surprised.

"Oh, no," replied the khan, "to Lahore (in the Pakistani Punjab). Anything the other side of the Indus is 'Hindustan' to our people."

The khan decided to accompany us on our trip westwards through Mardan District. He took us first to Shabaz Ghari, a village not far from the town of Mardan. Here we fell in with a class of schoolboys. Their teacher was taking them to see the famous rock inscriptions carved by the Buddhist emperor Asoka in the third century before Christ. We scrambled about the rocks together and all posed for a picture in front of the ancient emperor's plea for peace and morality among men.

We stood atop the largest rock and looked down over the fertile Mardan Plain. The teacher pointed out his village lying in a blue haze amidst fields of young wheat. He gave us a brief account of Asoka's reign which, when I later checked it in a monumental history, proved remarkably accurate. He spoke with the calm self-confidence and slightly aloof courtesy typical of the Pathans, indicating his awareness of our companion's status by calling him 'khan'. He referred to me politely as 'the sahib', and paid Edith the unusual compliment of 'Begum Sahiba' rather than 'Memsahib', the form usually used to Western women by servants and tradesmen in most of Pakistan and India.

As we turned to leave he relaxed a little. "They say in our

village that Asoka came there too," he said with a trace of a smile. "Why else would he have felt it necessary to take the great trouble of carving this praise of peace and good behaviour on these rocks?"

My objective in the town of Mardan was the library of the Yusufzai khans of Hoti. I had heard of a large collection of books, many of them local history, which had been acquired by Nawab Sir Akbar Khan of Hoti before his death a few years ago. I had no plan as to how to gain access to the library and intended when I arrived to look up the local deputy-commissioner and explain my purpose.

I mentioned this to the Zaida Khan as we neared Mardan. "Capital! Capital!" he said. "We will stay there. It will take you a few days to look over the books and I have not seen the Hotis for a long time."

Not without doubts as to the propriety of the incursion, we allowed him to direct us through the gate of a vast building surrounding a central courtyard. A horde of servants appeared. After only the briefest exchange with our guide, they led us to a suite of rooms on the ground floor. We dispatched one of them to the telegraph office with a series of messages rearranging our future itinerary.

The furniture was Victorian, dark and massive. The beds all had canopies. A humidor of Havana cigars, dusty and crumbling, stood on one table. A combination cigarette-box, lighter, and ash-tray in the shape of a First World War French tank, graced another. A lance leaned in a corner of the bathroom, handy to the tub. Edith found this a very amusing bit of interior decoration, until she was told it was "for cobras" which attracted by the water like to slide into bathrooms.

We were, our friend explained, in the 'old' house. The library was here, but the Hoti brothers lived a quarter of a mile away in the 'new' house. The place we were in had seventy-two rooms; the other, somewhat more . . . "excluding the women's quarters, of course".

The breakfast table next morning was twenty feet long and set for as many persons. Edith and I faced our friend and the khan of Hoti across the centre of it.

We were alone, except for an occasional servant bringing food, and four solemn bearded men, revolvers and cartridge belts

strapped to their waists, who stood behind our chairs. Their duty
it appeared later on was to swing fly-whisks while we enjoyed
our breakfasts. We discovered later that the khan had just become
deeply involved in a family quarrel with his brothers. Indeed our
host, the eldest of the five sons of the old nawab, was subsequently
unseated as head of the family. Under the circumstances our arrival
must have been an unwelcome distraction.

None of this was evident, however, as he welcomed us
graciously and chatted with our companion about his boyhood
days. He indicated that he cherished the library because it was his
father's, but that neither he nor his brothers made any use of it or
indeed had much knowledge about it. However, he gave me
carte blanche to do anything I wanted in the library, apologised
that he would not be able to be in personal attendance on us, and
departed.

The library was impressive, albeit rather dusty. There were
three or four 'librarians' in attendance. Alone among the men of
the household, they were not armed. There was no evidence that
anyone had opened a book since the death of the old nawab a few
years earlier. However, shipments of books still arrived from all
over the World in fulfilment of the standing orders he had left
before his death. The chief duty of the 'librarians' seemed to be
uncrating these shipments and 'cataloguing' them—in hand-
written notebooks in the order of acquisition.

I worked through half a dozen rooms which must have contained virtually every book ever published in any European
language or in Pushtu, Urdu, and Persian which had to do with
the Frontier. Other rooms housed the late nawab's superb collection of works on military history. We were shown original Pushtu
manuscripts of the works of the great Pushtu poet Khushal Khan
Khattak, a large selection of the classic works of Islam in manuscript form from the library of the amir of Bokhara, and priceless
Arabic manuscripts, including one of Euclid's works which was
more than a thousand years old.

We had been the first visitors to the library in more than a
year we were told, and when we left the rusty bolts on the great
wooden doors were shut once more.

IX

Mohmands and Mohammadzai

ONE OF the Mohmands' favourite stories is of a venerable member of their tribe who lay dying. He had lived long, worked hard, and owned many acres. As he prepared for his final rest he was surrounded by his stalwart sons, to whom would pass his land and the obligation of carrying on the honour of the clan.

As is promised by Islam to the faithful, the Angel of Death appeared. With him the Angel had the book in which he inscribes the names of those who enter Paradise.

"What is your name, Malik Sahib?" the Angel asked the dying man.

"Ah, here you are," said the old Mohmand. "Tell me, Holy One, is there any good land I can buy in Paradise?"

The Angel smiled. "Your name, Brother, for the Book of the Blessed?" he repeated.

"Well, if there is no good land, perhaps I could buy some poor land and improve it," said the old man.

"Your name?" insisted the Angel.

"If there is no land left to buy, I will be satisfied to rent some good land," countered the Mohmand.

"Your name!"

"Maybe there is some poor land I could rent?"

"Your name!"

"Well," persisted the dying Mohmand, "if there is none to rent, you must at least have some I could sharecrop."

The moral of the story is that whenever a Mohmand comes into a new place, his first thought is for land.

In all there are more than 200,000 Mohmands, about half of whom live in Pakistan and half in Afghanistan. Most of those in Pakistan live in tribal territory in an area of about a thousand square miles north of the Khyber and the Kabul River. The country is hilly and inaccessible. Needless to say, there has never

6

been enough arable land in it to satisfy the Mohmands' insatiable hunger for the soil.

Many of them have encroached on the plains and by virtue of their inexhaustible energy and ability as husbandmen have won title to fertile acres from the less energetic Pathans of the settled areas. A particularly bustling colony of Mohmands has grown up at the expense of the Yusufzai khans along the Lower Swat Canal in Mardan District.

I have lived for happy weeks in one of these villages, staying in a *hujra* (guest-house) second only to the Wali of Swat's hotel in comfort and appointments. The two brothers, both in their thirties, who own much of the surrounding land, are remarkable in many ways. Both have travelled in Europe and America. They are completely and intensely loyal to each other, and the bitter fraternal feuds which have riven many Pathan families are absent here. The eldest is the first member of his tribe ever to obtain a college degree. He devotes himself to public life, working to promote the political and economic interests of the Mohmands settled about the Yusufzai country and striving to maintain his influence among the Mohmands in the hills from which his father and grandfather migrated almost half a century ago. Both brothers lend a hand themselves in the fields at harvest time—a most unusual phenomenon for the Pathan gentry. However, it is the younger brother who oversees the day-to-day running of the land—who finds his satisfaction in making the fields produce their rich yield and in providing the money that 'Lala' (elder brother) expends on his multifarious causes.

Their village lies a mile or two off the Mardan–Malakand road, just across from the town of Takht-i-Bhai, noted locally for its sugar-refinery and internationally for the ruins of an ancient Buddhist monastery. The road to the village is barely wide enough for a single car. It is lined with young poplar-trees which stand like an immensely tall picket-fence over the tightly-packed, man-high sugar-cane which crowd the fields.

The road comes to a full stop at a tall, whitewashed adobe wall. Within the square of the wall live the dozens of people, relatives, retainers, and servants, who make up the household of the brothers. Access to the interior is by a single heavy wooden door. Outside the wall are a few sheds for cars, trucks, and farm machinery. Several acres of garden stretch away beyond the outbuildings until the ever-present sugar-cane stands square against the horizon.

The Pathans' devotion to their gardens is a characteristic inherited from their Central Asian forebears. This garden is dominated by an enormous shishim-tree, larger than the greatest oak. In its shade water runs gently between rows of fruit-trees, apple, peach, pear, orange, guava, and persimmon.

The atmosphere of the garden is peaceful. Yet even here one is never allowed to forget the note of danger and insecurity which —not unpleasantly—underlies life on the Frontier. The garden is outside the walls and those who stroll in it must be protected. When the brothers take their evening stroll a few tribesmen with rifles on their shoulders follow at a discreet distance. When I wandered into the garden to read or nap an armed figure appeared, to offer a pillow for my head or to peel my apple. Inevitably, he managed to remain in attendance until I returned to the safety of the walls.

Indeed, one of the first things the visitor to the Frontier notes is that he is hardly ever alone. If he is a person of any consequence he must be prepared to hold *durbar* almost in the manner of the Mogul emperors. At any hour the friendly and curious will come to see and talk with him. To reject them is to be unworthy of his status. If he is a guest he must be attended upon and protected constantly by his host. 'The position' must be determined—how he is, where he has been, what he wants to do. 'The programme' —where he is to go and whom he is to see—must be discussed and agreed upon.

This public rôle is not reserved for the stranger. Even the least important of the Pathan *maliks* and khans lives in an atmosphere similar to that which surrounds presidents and prime ministers in the West. When he leaves the house, he must always be accompanied by a few relatives and armed retainers to protect him and to give him stature. He must spend a portion of every day in his *hujra* to welcome visitors and to discuss the events of the day with his peers and dependants. Even in the sacrosanct *zennana* (women's quarters) he is likely to be alone only in his maleness, being surrounded by his mother, assorted sisters, aunts and female cousins, as well as his wife (or wives) and children (usually numerous).

This highly public way of living can at first be a trial to the

Westerner accustomed to a more private mode of existence. The various Europeans who pushed into Central Asia in the nineteenth century were frequently driven to the edge of insanity by the insatiable and uninhibited intimacy which was forced upon them by their Turkoman, Uzbek, Tajik and Kirghiz hosts. This is not the case among the Pathans whose dignity and reserve soon make the visitor feel both important and at ease. After a day or two he is carrying off the rôle of a public figure with as much nonchalance and enjoyment as the most experienced *malik*. Indeed, the day he finds no one waiting outside his door, he begins to wonder if it is not time to move on to people more appreciative of his virtues and talents.

The gate in the wall of the Mohmand compound opens on to a wide expanse of green lawn. At one side is a low whitewashed adobe building with rough-hewn wooden door-frames and narrow windows. *Charpoys*, the simple country beds of India and Pakistan, are scattered about in front and crowd the rooms within. Here the *maliks'* dependants and friends gather. Many of them are tribesmen down from the hills to report on conditions among the home clan or merely to stop for a cup of tea on their way to Mardan or Peshawar. Their conversation is slow, and despite the harsh gutturals which plague the student just starting to learn Pushtu, it is soft in tone and volume. There are frequent pauses but the thread is never broken, and a day passed in talking is a day well spent.

The 'new' *hujra* dominates the far end of the compound. It is a long, high-ceilinged, rectangular building, equipped with sitting-room, dining-room, several bedrooms, and bathroom complete with Western-style fixtures. The important business of the brothers and their village is carried on on the wide veranda which crosses the front of the 'new' *hujra*. At such times, the faded blue turbans and dusty shirts of the tribesmen mingle with the lounge-suits of Government officials and the smart uniforms of an occasional police or army officer; the low hum of everyday conversation becomes a muted roar as positions are presented and arguments made for new irrigation ditches or increased quotas of sugar-cane for the mill.

The family home adjoins both *hujras* in the rear. It is a three-storey structure built around a central tower and decorated in the old style with wooden latticed purda balconies from which the ladies of the house can catch a glimpse of the proceedings below and check up on the elaborate establishment they daily supply with the plentiful food and conveniences their men take for granted.

Life has prospered for a long time in the fields that surround the little town of Takht-i-Bhai. A few years ago, while levelling ground for a new set of houses for tenant farmers, the brothers came upon a mass of shattered sculpture from the Buddhist period about the time of Christ when the Peshawar Valley was known as Gandhara, 'the Garden Land'.

Being devout Muslims, they placed little value on the delicately carved figures of black schist which the spades of the workmen uncovered. The workmen, also devout Muslims, had even less respect for the 'idols'. They smashed at the remains of Buddhas and Bodhisattvas with glee and most of the broken stone figures were pulverised to provide rubble for the foundations of the new huts. I arrived in time to salvage a few remnants and later led a party of Fulbright professors to pick over the heaps of rubble for souvenirs of a kind not readily available in the shops of Lahore and Karachi.

The site which now lies beneath the bright and sanitary new huts of the tenant farmers were probably a small shrine, an off-shoot of the great monastery whose ruins still run for a mile along the top of a steep outcropping of rock just the other side of the modern village of Takht-i-Bhai. The first excavations at Takht-i-Bhai were done in 1871 and much of the Gandhara sculpture in the museums of Europe and America, as well as those in Peshawar and Lahore, was found at this site.

To the layman, the most interesting aspect of this sculpture is its obvious combination of Greek and Indian elements. The subject-matter is Buddhist and Indian. Yet the features and the hairdress, the drapery of the garments, and the classic proportions of heads, limbs, and torsos are all unmistakably Hellenic. There is one small head in the Peshawar Museum which I recognised instantly as being virtually identical with the traditional bust of Aristotle which appeared in my high-school history book.

Despite the profusion of riches which has been unearthed at Takht-i-Bhai, relatively little is known of the origins of the monastic community. Its size and high state of development, together with its location in the very heart of ancient Gandhara,

make it obvious that it was a major cultural centre. Yet the inde-
fatigable Chinese Buddhist pilgrims, Fa Hien and Hiuen Tsang,
who passed through Gandhara in the fifth and seventh centuries
AD and left detailed accounts of their travels, make no mention
of Takht-i-Bhai.

There is one fact, however, which ties Takht-i-Bhai in a real
and intimate way to the pattern of history with which we are
familiar in the West. Among the shattered Buddhas was found a
rock inscription (now in the Lahore Museum) dating the reign
of the great king Gondophares from AD 19 to AD 46. This
confirmed the existence of this Parthian ruler of northern India
whose name in its Armenian form, Gaspar, is that of one of the
wise men of the East who came to Palestine at the time of the
birth of Christ.

Gondophares appears also as Gudnaphar in the apocryphal *Acts
of Judas Thomas the Apostle*, which dates at least to the third
century AD.

The apocryphal *Acts* give a colourful account of how India fell
to Thomas when the Apostles were casting lots for missionary
territory. Thomas refused to go, saying, "I have not strength
enough. Besides I am a Jew. How can I teach Indians?" Then the
risen Lord appeared to Thomas and said: "Fear not, Thomas, my
grace will be with you." But Thomas still refused, answering,
"Whithersoever Thou willst, Lord, send me; only to India I will
not go."

There then arrived on the scene an Indian merchant named
Habban who was seeking a skilled carpenter to bring back to
King Gudnaphar in India. The Lord appeared again and sold
Thomas to Habban whom he accompanied back to India where
he was appointed to construct a new palace for Gondophares.
Thomas spent the money he was given for the palace on works
of charity in the King's name. When Gondophares discovered
this, Thomas was cast into prison. Meanwhile the King's brother
died and was taken into heaven where he saw the celestial palace
that Thomas had built for Gondophares through his good works.
Whereupon the King's brother was restored to life and both he
and Gondophares were converted to Christianity. Later Thomas
met a martyr's death in South India where large numbers of
Indian Christians still claim descent from his original converts.

Gondophares had been long dead—and, one hopes, enjoying

the fruits of Thomas's labours—when the Mohmand brothers took us on a picnic to the monastery. Accompanied by cousins and nephews, drivers and guards, our convoy of Jeeps bumped across the rough plain to the bottom of the rock spur on which the ruins perch. On foot we climbed about 1,500 feet along a narrow path. Rifles bounced against vacuum flasks as our companions moved along. A short fat cousin led the way. Bandoliers crossed his chest. A rifle was slung on one shoulder, its butt barely clearing the ground. Two revolvers and a knife snuggled in his ample waistband. He clutched a wicker-basket of delicacies under one arm. Sweat poured from beneath his flat wool Chitrali cap, but he managed to maintain a wide and unfailing grin even while panting from the exertions of the climb. Towards the top, he climbed ahead to make sure all was in order above.

The sight which met our eyes when we emerged through the ruined walls of the monastery into the great forecourt would have delighted Gondophares. The ground was strewn with carpets. Tables spread with white cloths and decorated with flowers and great mounds of fruit were scattered about. Servants broiled chickens over a series of small fires in one corner. A dozen men, most of them in typical Pathan dress, rose to greet us. Off to one side, the custodian of the ruins stood scratching his head, not sure that the regulations of the Archaeological Survey permitted the cavalier appropriation of such historic grounds for an outing.

Nevertheless, after we had shaken hands all around, he took us on a tour of the monastery, pointing out with the superiority of a follower of the one true God the places where the 'idolators' had prayed, slept, eaten, and studied. We soon gave over the wonders of the past for the delights of the present and attacked the food. Dozens of different curries and pillaus were available in huge china bowls and we sampled them all. To her amazement, Edith consumed two of the chickens, and I managed three. Between us, we did away with a dozen blood oranges whose rich red fruit is a local delicacy at certain seasons of the year.

The polite egalitarianism which characterises Pathan manners was evident during the meal. Everyone dipped into every dish. Servants and retainers were deferential but helped themselves and entered freely into the conversation. The old custodian and an anonymous member of the Mohmand party engaged in a lengthy debate as to whether or not the 'idol-worshippers' who originally inhabited Takht-i-Bhai were 'bad people' in so far as they had lived before the time of the Holy Prophet of Islam.

I offered the not altogether pertinent comment that Christians believed that the Jewish religion was the true one before the coming of Christ. The debating pair nodded sagely and reminded me that the Pathans were descended from the tribes of Israel. The last word sparked off bitter remarks from other members of the company about the present-day state of Israel and US support for it. One of the *maliks* led the conversation away from this sensitive subject by suggesting that we talk of happier things, Kashmir, for instance.

I had frequently heard Pathans complaining about American failure to give Pakistan unqualified support in its quarrel with India over the princely state and was not aware that the subject of Kashmir was a particularly happy one. However, it was personal reminiscences rather than political causes that the *malik* had in mind. He had been on the Kashmir *jihad* in 1947 and many of those present had been with him.

A young tribesman, who, judging from his looks, could have been no more than fourteen in 1947, proudly showed the rifle he had captured from a soldier of the Kashmiri maharaja. "I took also two big boxes of ammunition which the *malik sahib* still keeps for me," the boy explained. In a style reminiscent of Hemingway, an old man told of how, after a clash with a party of Sikhs, he had fought in the snow, walking for three days in his bare feet and living on two pieces of *nan*, the flat round bread of the Pathans. His eyes began to flash as he exclaimed that he must return to Kashmir to avenge the injuries he had suffered. The *malik* cut him off gently. "It was a good time, *Lala*; we went along singing, with our rifles in our hands, and nothing could stand before us."

The manager of the local sugar-mill, a highly Westernised refugee from India, appeared as we sat talking. With him was his guest, a young Swiss businessman. Both of them were welcomed to the meal. In the course of the conversation the Swiss extolled the undoubted superiority of his people, including himself, in the fields of mountain climbing and shooting. With a twinkle in their eyes, a pair of young tribesmen offered to show him a part of the Buddhist ruin farther along the crest of the spur. I indicated a desire to come too, but sensed a note of reluctance in their agreement and withdrew.

In half an hour we saw the trio crawling about on a pile of rubble perched precariously on the rocky ridge half a mile away. Ten minutes later the two tribesmen were back, smug but silent. After an hour the distraught Swiss re-appeared, his trousers torn, his arms and legs scratched, obviously surprised to be still alive. His guides expressed concern and solicitude, indicating that they had thought he must be right behind them all the way.

Re-assured by several cups of green tea and profuse compliments on his dexterity and daring, the Swiss let himself be drawn into a round of rifle shooting with the rest of us. A retainer was dispatched to plant a handkerchief on a side of the spur several hundred yards opposite the monastery. I was delighted that my marksmanship was not much worse than that of the *maliks* and their tribesmen who preceded me. Edith performed nobly, raising a puff of dust a few feet from the white target. Her chagrin at missing was tempered by an old man's remark, interpreted by one of the *maliks*: "Tell her she does well. That target is very small. If it had been a man, she would have hit him, and that is all that counts."

The Swiss was determined to uphold his national honour. He took the ·303 Enfield which a tribesman handed him and looked it over carefully. Taking up his stance at one side where he could rest the rifle on a wall, he wet his finger to determine the direction of the wind and adjusted the sights for range. After fully five minutes of aiming, he squeezed the trigger. Nothing happened. A tribesman solemnly reached over and flicked off the safety catch.

Muttering, the marksman repeated his lengthy process of aiming and once again pressed the trigger. Still nothing. The tribesman took the rifle and, with apologies, injected a shell into the empty chamber. On the third try the rifle fired. We all peered at the hill opposite but no puff of dust was evident. After some debate, it was agreed that he must have hit right in the centre of the handkerchief which muffled the dust, and all crowded around to congratulate him, their respect apparently restored.

Later, on the way down the hill, the tribesman who was walking next to me pulled an ammunition clip from his bandolier. He passed it to me and with a wordless grin gestured at the Swiss who was trudging along in front of us. The brass cartridge case at the top of the clip contained the usual powder charge held in place by a paper tab, but the pointed steel bullet was lacking. It was a country-made blank which the Pathans shoot off to celebrate festive occasions.

One can return to Peshawar from Takht-i-Bhai by a back-road which runs through the town of Charsadda. This road is narrow and winding. There is little vehicular traffic to be met on it. Sugar-cane comes down to its edge in many places. In others, it runs between groves of tamarisks. Here and there the yellow earth is exposed in deep *nullas*, or gulleys. Cane, trees, and *nullas* are all excellent for ambush, and scenes in more than one Pathan feud have been played out here.

The countryside opens up a mile or two before one reaches Charsadda, and off to the right lies the Mohammadzai village of Utmanzai. The Mohammadzai are a comparatively small and well-settled Pathan clan whose habits and customs are similar to those of the Yusufzai. Utmanzai is the home of the famous Khan brothers whose names have figured prominently for the last thirty years in the fiery politics of the subcontinent.

Dr Khan Sahib began his career as a member of the Indian medical service and ended it a few years ago at the hands of an assassin in Lahore after he had resigned as Chief Minister of West Pakistan. Paradoxically, for he and his brother were both Muslim and Pathan, he had spent most of his political life as a member of the Hindu-dominated Congress Party of Gandhi and Nehru.

The real paradox of Utmanzai, however, is Abdul Ghaffar Khan, widely known before 1947 as 'the Frontier Gandhi', and an intimate associate of Jawaharlal Nehru, the Kashmiri Brahmin, and Mohendas Gandhi, the Gujerati *bania*. Abdul Ghaffar Khan's great creation was the *Khudai Khitmatgars*, 'the Servants of God', which he founded in 1929 to fight British rule in India. The *Khudai Khitmatgars* provided a uniform for themselves by dyeing their shirts with local brick dust. British officialdom, which suspected that there must be something communistic about the organisation anyway, dubbed them 'the Red Shirts', and as such they have been known ever since.

Abdul Ghaffar Khan never relented in his fight with the British and lost no time in 1947 in throwing down the gauntlet to the new Muslim League government of Pakistan which had inherited sovereignty over the Frontier from the British. The referendum in which the people of the North-West Frontier Province had chosen Pakistan over India was a fraud, said Abdul Ghaffar Khan. The real choice of the Pathans was independence, and this had not been offered them. His demands for an autonomous 'Pushtoonistan' or 'Pathanistan' were supported by Afghanistan, to whom much of the Frontier had once belonged, and a stormy political conflict got under way.

Ghaffar Khan lost. He has spent at least half of his life since 1947 in Pakistani jails. When he was released in 1954 (he has been re-arrested several times since) he was forbidden to return to the Frontier, and I first met him not at Utmanzai but at Karachi.

The meeting had been arranged by a prominent Pathan friend who confessed to have a considerable admiration for Ghaffar Khan but had no desire to be seen in public with him. My friend took me to a point near one of Karachi's worst refugee settlements. He pointed at a run-down Pakistani-style hotel down the street. "You will find the Badshah Khan (literally, 'Great Khan of Khans') there," he said, and hurried off.

A relative and associate of Abdul Ghaffar was waiting for me inside the hotel courtyard. He took me up to a small room on the third floor and offered to serve as interpreter, saying that the Badshah Khan did not speak English. Outside the door two poorly dressed Pathans sat cross-legged. They regarded me with blank, indifferent eyes and, uncharacteristically, did not respond to my greeting.

We found Abdul Ghaffar Khan lying on a rumpled bed. Tall and gaunt, he looked like a sick Jeremiah outside the gates of a king of Israel. He wore a single long garment of homespun, something like an old-fashioned nightshirt, and his grizzled head was bare. Above his prominent Pathan nose huge dark eyes glistened and charged the otherwise dim and dingy room with a sense of urgency. He did not rise but offered me his hand; he gripped mine so strongly that I was unable to withdraw it and had to slip into the chair pushed gently against the back of my knees by his associate.

Still holding my hand, he stared into my eyes and asked in Pushtu, "What do you want to know about my poor people, the Pathans?"

I told him I was interested in everything about the Pathans but at the moment was most interested in himself and his political ideas. I added that while many of the Pathans I had met were poor in material things, I thought them all proud and rich in spirit.

"Yes," he agreed. "We are a proud people despite all the oppression we have suffered, first from the British and now from these *babus* (an opprobrious term usually applied to government clerks) who call themselves Pakistanis. Freedom to live our own lives, that is all we want. Yet they call us traitors and say I am disloyal. I am loyal to my people. That is all I will be loyal to. You Americans should help us, instead of listening only to these people in Karachi," he added. "The Russians should help us. We welcome you all."

"Does this freedom you want have to be outside of Pakistan?" I asked. "Can you not be free within Pakistan?"

"This is a matter of no importance," Ghaffar Khan insisted. "What matters is that we be free to develop ourselves, to tear down our own khans who have oppressed us, to make our own laws, to speak our own language. For this they say I am an agent of Afghanistan. For this they call me traitor. It is false! I have never opposed Pakistan."

His associate chimed in to deny that the Badshah Khan had ever wanted to take the Pathans out of Pakistan. He pressed upon me a copy of a letter he said Ghaffar had sent to the Pakistani authorities from prison protesting that his demands were only for an autonomous province within Pakistan.

I found this difficult to believe. I had studied carefully the record of Abdul Ghaffar Khan's activities before and at the time of Partition. I knew that even after he had been released from prison in 1954, unlike his brother Khan Sahib, he consistently avoided making the unequivocal declaration of loyalty which would probably have restored him to a position of honour and prestige in Pakistan. I knew that he had done nothing to oppose the propaganda from Afghanistan which demands an independent 'Pushtoonistan' and which idolises him as a national leader.

Yet it was hard to hold fast to these facts in the full blaze of the old man's personality. To my surprise he had slipped into English after our first few words. His vocabulary seemed not to exceed a few hundred words but he used them with extraordinary force and all the skill of a polished orator. He dropped my hand to spread forth his arms in an impassioned plea for freedom. He took it again to demonstrate the sincerity of his denial of being an Afghan agent. It was easy to imagine the impact he would have, speaking in Pushtu, on an audience of Pathans, great admirers of the spoken word.

We talked for two hours. Towards the end he lapsed into Pushtu again. Finally with a smile, half-sad, half-sardonic, he dismissed me with the traditional benediction, *"Pa mukha dai khuh"*. I could feel his burning eyes on my back as I walked through the door.

Ghaffar Khan's relative escorted me to the hotel gate. As we passed through the compound, a policeman sitting at a table against the wall called to us in Urdu. My companion went over and spoke to him. They argued over an entry in the policeman's book. After a few minutes Ghaffar Khan's relative returned to me.

"Excuse me, sir," he said. "The constable is not sure he has your name spelled right on his list. Do you have a calling card we could give him?"

X

Kurrum and Kohat

THE DISTRICT of Kohat lies to the south of Peshawar. Kurrum Agency is adjacent to it on the west. The first few times I visited Kohat I thought of it simply as an area one had to go through when passing between such intriguing places as the Khyber and Waziristan. As for Kurrum, I knew it to be the most settled and peaceful part of the tribal territory and had never bothered to visit it at all. It took a mild-mannered poet who abhorred arms and bloodshed to teach me otherwise.

Mian Sahib, though still young in years, was an intellectual of the old school. He had achieved local fame as a Pushtu poet and had served occasionally at Pakistani embassies abroad. He invariably wore a grey karakul cap and a rusty black suit of vaguely British cut. He adjusted to the seasons and to the days' variations in temperature by adding or subtracting a grey woollen sweater. He was a gentle man, given to long periods of silence. When he spoke, it was usually to quote from the colourful collection of Eastern and Western poets whose venerable sayings seemed more alive in his mind than the bustling life of the Frontier around him.

When I met him, Mian Sahib was putting in a stint as Director of Tribal Publicity. I had been badgering the authorities for permission to visit a particularly inaccessible part of tribal territory. Perhaps to divert me and perhaps merely because he wanted a companion, Mian Sahib suggested I accompany him on a tour of Kurrum and Kohat. We set off from Peshawar on a crisp autumn morning and within an hour were in the town of Kohat.

My wife had commissioned me to get her a pair of the leather sandals that are the speciality of the town. Mian Sahib happily turned aside from his official business to help me hunt for slippers. Clutching a piece of paper on which the outline of Edith's foot was prominently inscribed, we began a round of visits to the shoe-stalls in the Kohat bazaar. The peculiar Kohat sandals were there, all right, thousands of them, all variations of the same design with a broad triangular instep guard. Sandals were to be had in red and green, black and gold, yellow and purple. They sported red pom-poms, green pom-poms, white pom-poms, and black pom-poms. They were in every size from three inches long to two inches shorter than I needed.

I patiently displayed my outline. The first shopkeeper merely looked and shook his head sadly. The next got out a yardstick (incongruously marked 'Bargain Paint Co.') and measured what he obviously considered a giant footprint. He then shrugged hopelessly. Another, of a more commercial turn of mind, insisted that his largest sandals (fully three inches shorter than required) would be a perfect fit. The last one studied the outline and pushed it back with the laconic comment: "My sandals only for ladies, Sahib."

We finally abandoned the venture and my piece of paper to a particularly energetic cobbler who offered to make sandals in the required size which we could pick up some days later on our return through Kohat. (He made the sandals, all right, one inch too short, and for only two rupees extra.)

Mian Sahib now announced it was lunch-time and, in an obviously not-unconnected suggestion, proposed we call upon the deputy commissioner. The deputy commissioner and his wife turned out to be in Peshawar, but with typical Frontier informality we inspected his garden and house. The house, built three-quarters of a century earlier by Sir Louis Cavagnari before his death in the massacre of the British in Kabul during the Second Afghan War, is an architectural gem. Modelled after Thomas Jefferson's house at Monticello, Virginia, it has an airy grace and elegance despite its thick walls and high windows. The tile floors were spread with magnificent oriental carpets. Bearded tribesmen squatted patiently in the shade of the garden while troops of brightly dressed children, ever present in Pakistan, frolicked among them. It was obvious that Kohat was at peace and that political affairs pressed lightly, for the moment at least, upon the head of the district.

Mian Sahib declined an offer of lunch from the servants. "So-o-o-o," he said, "we go to the bazaar."

Back in the bazaar, he led the way up a steep flight of stone steps, less than two feet wide. We emerged on the balcony, scarcely wider, of what Mian Sahib told me was Kohat's premier eating-house. A dozen feet below, the life of the Kohat bazaar went on. Vendors and customers pushed their way between swarms of careening bicycles. Teams of tiny donkeys, heads bobbing and bells jingling, trotted in and out. Occasionally a disdainful camel plodded by, its malevolent eyes almost on a level with our table.

Mian Sahib ignored the tumult. He gave our order to the waiter with as much care as if he were composing an epic. Glasses of 'sherbet', iced pomegranate juice, arrived at once. A good while later came a large pot of green tea. Finally the waiter presented a huge pewter salwar heaped with *kebabs*.

"*Chapli kebab, shami kebab, sikhi kebab*," he explained. To complete the repast, he tossed on to the table half a dozen large flat rounds of the Pathan bread, called *nan*. A few minutes later he was back to offer me a battered soup-spoon and an ancient two-pronged fork.

It is easy enough to describe a *kebab* as ground meat mixed with spices. To convey an impression of the flavour, however, is as difficult as it is to interpret the spirit of the East. The *chapli kebab* is large. Its name comes from the heavy leather sandals that the Pathans wear called *chaplis*, and its size corresponds to what would be the sole of a big shoe. Being big, it is not considered necessary to grind the spices that go into it and I found myself chewing on a whole chilli pepper. This is an experience to be remembered.

When my ravaged mouth had been somewhat soothed by another pomegranate sherbet, we left Kohat for Kurrum Agency. The road winds westwards through the town of Hangu, where the Mogul emperor Babur erected a pillar of Pathan heads. The countryside is arid, near desert in places, but occasional fields and clumps of trees began to appear as we neared Thal, at the mouth of the Kurrum Valley.

Thal was crowded with *powendas*, the nomad Ghilzai Pathans. The police-station where we stopped to announce our presence was a scene of bustling confusion. *Powendas* jammed the veranda, their camels placidly standing or sitting hip-to-hip in the courtyard. The hall inside was lined on both sides with more *powendas*, all straining to hear what was going on in the inspector's office. When we pushed our way into the office, we found another dozen *powendas*, all shouting simultaneously at the inspector.

The subject of the argument, it turned out, was the *powendas'* guns. They had been relieved of their armament when they crossed the Afghan border at the head of the Kurrum Valley. They had been given claim checks which they were to present the next spring when they were returning to Afghanistan in order to receive back their weapons. On the way down the valley this particular group had decided they would return in the spring by another route. Now they wanted their guns back.

The inspector interrupted the debate long enough to shake hands with us and wish us godspeed. "It's a pleasure to have some-one going *up* the valley these days," he said.

As we drove out of Thal to the westward, Mian Sahib looked pensively at the caravans straggling towards us along the road and the *powenda* encampments which crowded every flat place along the route. "Everyone talks about the Khyber," he said, "but this is the way a sensible man would invade. The terrain is better. There are fewer forts. There's water all the way down. The people in the valley are peaceful, not like the Afridis in the Khyber."

As a matter of fact, the Kurrum Valley was the invasion route chosen by one of the most sensible of all Afghans, Nadir Khan, the most recent in the long and illustrious line of invaders of India. How he came to do so and what happened to him after-wards is a tale full of daring and intrigue of the kind that delights the heart of the Pathans.

In 1919 the Amir Habibulla of Afghanistan was assassinated. He was succeeded by his son, the youthful Amanulla. Beset by numerous pretenders to the throne and widespread unrest within his country, Amanulla rallied all Afghans by the simple expedient of declaring war on India. There was little fighting and the war was over in scarcely more than a month. But during that eventful May of 1919 Amanulla's general, Nadir Khan, had swept down the Kurrum and occupied Thal for a few hours. Ten years later Amanulla was driven from his throne by a tribal revolt, and was succeeded by the same Nadir Khan, father of the present king, Zahir Shah of Afghanistan. Nadir was assassinated in 1933. Amanulla lived on, exiled in Italy, until 1960, when he died peacefully in his bed.

The drive up the Kurrum Valley reminds one of the Swat Valley. These are virtually the only ribbons of fertility in the

7

entire tribal area. In the lower Kurrum both sides of the river are dotted with fields of artemesia, a medicinal plant which goes into the make-up of such varied compounds as santonin (a specific for intestinal worms) and absinthe (a panacea for other ills). A dwarf palm, called *mazari*, the fibres of which are made into sandals and baskets by the tribesmen, covers the slopes of the hills. At two points lines of saw-tooth tank-traps stretch across the wide river-bed.

Farther up there are groves of enormously tall *chinar* (plane) trees, reminiscent of California redwoods. The villages lie in the shadow of the *chinars*. Icy streams on their way to the Kurrum run between the adobe houses and bring coolness and music to the inhabitants.

We stopped in one village at a little tea-shop built like a tiny covered bridge across a rivulet. The proprietor washed the cups by reaching down through a hole in the floor to immerse them in the rushing water. He filled his copper kettle in the same manner. While waiting for it to boil, he offered us slices of the peculiar peach-like fruit which is unique to the upper Kurrum Valley.

I noticed that three cups stood on the tray that he was preparing and assumed that the proprietor intended to join us, since there was no one else in sight save a pair of wide-eyed children. He removed the pot from the fire and poured the tea. The third cup was half full when an old man appeared from the far bank and with casual grace seated himself opposite us.

It seemed to me that the whole affair had the pre-arranged precision of a top Broadway production, but Mian Sahib gave no sign of surprise. He and the newcomer exchanged the classic Pathan greetings: "May you never be tired"; "May you never be in need." I added my welcome.

Without preamble, the old man raised an arm and gestured down the tree-lined path which ran beside the stream. He spoke for several minutes in sonorous Pushtu, pointing here and there with great emphasis, pausing occasionally for dramatic affect. At the end he put down his empty cup, rose abruptly but solemnly, shook hands, and departed.

I had caught parts of the story as he told it and Mian Sahib filled in the gaps. The tale was classic and simple. Once a great king had come alone down this path from Kabul. His name, some said, was Sher Shah; others insisted that it was Nadir Khan; but that was not important. Under a particularly tall *chinar*, a few dozen feet away, the king had seen a simple *powenda* girl washing clothes in the stream. He had been struck by her beauty, she by his manly bearing. He had lifted her on to his horse, taken her away, and made her his queen. That was all—save the fact that the old man had thought that I, being a stranger, should know of what happened here.

"That's charming," I said, "but who is this man who told us the story?"

"Him?" said Mian Sahib, paying for our tea, "nobody; just an old man."

Back in the car, riding up the shining valley, I decided that Mian Sahib's callousness was unworthy of him. "You claim you are a poet," I taxed him. "This old man told us a beautiful story, and from all I could make out, he told it beautifully. Yet you say he is nobody—just an old man. Don't you appreciate it at all?"

Mian Sahib was perplexed. "I appreciate it," he said. "As a matter of fact, it's true. It is written in several books which are very old. The old man, I think, lives in that village or another nearby. The tea-house man expected him, so I suppose he often comes to tell that tale to visitors. But I don't think he is very important. I did not recognise him and there were no other men with him. What more do you want me to say?"

"That's not what I mean," I said. "That story is obviously part of his life, part of a real folk culture. He told it very beautifully, like a poet or a troubadour."

"That's true," agreed Mian Sahib, still obviously puzzled, "but how else would a man tell a thing like that?"

The dominant tribe in the upper Kurrum is the Turis, who are in many ways distinct from the majority of Pathans. In the first place they are Shia Muslims; most Pathans are Sunnis. This has made a big difference in their lives. For one thing, it has meant that they have suffered considerable persecution from their more numerous Sunni neighbours. This in turn led them to do another thing which makes them unique among the Pathans. At an early date they invited the British to take over their territory in the hope that this would afford them some protection.

A few miles below Parachinar, which lies at the head of the

valley, a group of Turis appeared in the middle of the road and
stopped our car. It turned out that they had noticed the Government licence plate and assumed that we were high officials on
tour. They had a complaint about the political agent and wanted
him removed from office immediately. The complaint seemed to
centre on some technical detail of the marketing of their artemesia
crop. While Mian Sahib strove to convince them that neither he
nor I had any responsibility in the matter, I studied the faces
which crowded about the car windows.

They were more like what one would expect to find in Mukden
or Alma Alta than in Pakistan. Their eyes had the typical oriental
air of inscrutability given by the Mongol fold. High cheek bones
accentuated heart-shaped Tatar faces. Most chins were beardless.
All of the men were slightly built and delicately boned, a notice-
able contrast to the usual Pathan type. None of them carried rifles,
an even greater contrast. Indeed, the only common note they
struck with the rest of Pathankind was that they were denouncing
authority in loud, categorical terms.

I have never been able to find a satisfactory explanation for the
physical distinctiveness of the Turis. Some connect them with the
Hazaras of central Afghanistan as left-overs from the Mongol
invasions of Jenghis Khan and his sons. Others tie them to the
Kirghiz and the people from the neighbourhood of Kashgar, an
area with which the Frontier has had contact.

The Turis themselves claim descent from a Turkish family, the
Toghani, who migrated eastwards from Persia. While thoroughly
Pathan in culture, they preserve traces of a tribal code of their
own, called *Turizuna*, which, in addition to the provisions of
Pukhtunwali, provides for allegiance of each Turi clan to one of
the four families of saints who lived at scattered spots in the
valley.

At any rate, Mian Sahib managed to convince the disgruntled
tribesmen that we could not help them with their artemesia
problem and we were permitted to drive on to Parachinar, headquarters of the Kurrum Agency. Here we discovered that the
Kurrum Political Agent had also gone to Peshawar. However, we
were welcomed by an officer of the Kurrum Militia, the local
para-military unit, put up at the Government guest-house, and
invited for dinner at the Militia Mess that night.

Lounging on the veranda of the guest-house in the late afternoon, I looked out over a landscape remarkably like that of an Alpine village. The few double-storeyed houses scattered about were built of timber and stucco. Small, brilliantly green meadows, minute enough to be called terraces, ranged across the narrow valley, connecting with each other at the impossible angles one sees in a cluster of soap bubbles. 'The White Mountain', the last great peak of the Safed Koh, towered almost 16,000 feet into the sky, its snowcap flaming in the setting sun. The sun itself, not a neat yellow circle as it had been when high in the autumn sky a few hours earlier, but an angry, reddish-orange smear, spilled over the far side of the Paiwar Kotal Pass before burying itself in the wild central highlands of Afghanistan.

Dinner at the Mess, I discovered, was part of a one-hundred-year-old ritual. Mian Sahib (who had seemed to me to carry scarcely any luggage at all) appeared in a satin-lapelled, bow-tied version of his usual rusty black—complete with grey wool sweater. The colonel and the half-dozen officers who awaited us were resplendent in dress uniform. Tall candles and innumerable pieces of heavy silver decorated the table. Orderlies stood behind each chair. Trophies of battle and the hunt covered the walls so that only an occasional gleam of polished dark wood shone through.

My formal apology for my rumpled tweeds was formally accepted. I signed the guest-book and was offered whisky before and brandy after dinner, though none of the officers themselves indulged. The stately evening ended with a major offering to take me for a bird-shoot and a stroll about the border in the morning, and at nine o'clock I took myself back to four comforters and a roaring fire in the guest-house.

The birds failed to materialise the next morning, probably finding it too cold for even the most airy form of locomotion. When our blood had been warmed sufficiently by tramping to make thought and conversation feasible, the major took me up a hill for a look at the border. At his suggestion, we turned over our shot-guns to his orderly so as not to alarm the Afghan sentries when we appeared unexpectedly at the top of the crest. There, a quarter of a mile away and a few thousand feet below, was the border, marked by a straggling line of boundary posts. At the moment of our appearance, the line ran right through the centre of a long caravan of *powendas* heading into Pakistan. No one else was in sight, and the caravan gave no sign of being alarmed, or even of noticing, our presence.

Looking back into Pakistan, the major pointed to an airstrip which lay in the valley. "See that?" he asked. "Do you know how it was built?" I shook my head.

"Well," he explained, "that's the best spot in the valley—in fact, the only spot—for an airstrip. There was one problem, though, when the British wanted to build it there. There was a *pir*'s tomb right in the middle of that bit of ground."

I saw the problem. There are such tombs all over the Frontier, little stone monuments erected over the burial place, real or fancied, of a local *pir*, or saint. They are usually decorated with flags. Frequently, there is a little hut inhabited by a caretaker, who may be one of the *pir*'s descendants. The faithful visit, say their prayers, and sometimes leave small offerings to support the caretaker and to beautify the tomb.

This particular tomb, situated just below the Paiwar Kotal on one of the main routes through the Suleiman Mountains, must have been in a position to receive richer than usual offerings. To demolish it for the sake of infidel flying-machines would have grossly offended local sensibilities, both religious and economic, and would almost certainly have brought the local tribesmen screaming down against the British in *jihad*.

"So, what happened to the *pir*'s tomb?" I inquired.

The major smiled appreciatively. "There was a Pathan political officer," he said, "a very famous man he became later, but he was always clever. He did not live near here, but the British told him what they wanted, and one evening he came to the tomb, dressed as an ordinary tribesman. He stayed all night, saying his prayers and meditating. The next morning he left a generous offering and went away.

"That night he was back again. The caretaker saw him at his prayers and heard him invoking the spirit of the noble *pir* for guidance. In the morning he again left an offering and went away without a word.

"On the third night he came again to the tomb. By this time word of his pious behaviour had got about and a number of the local people had come to watch him at his devotions. He displayed great anxiety of spirit, and after a goodly crowd was gathered, he rose to leave. The people begged him to tell them of the purpose of his devotions. At first he was reluctant, but eventually let himself be persuaded.

" 'For many nights the *Pir Sahib* has appeared to me while I slept,' he explained. 'The *Pir Sahib* was troubled and in great pain, but I could not tell why. So I came here to pray at his tomb and to seek the reason for the affliction of so holy a man. It has now been made manifest to me why he sorrows, but, alas, I cannot do anything to help.'

"The people eagerly inquired as to what disturbed their *pir*.

" 'The holy saint's bones do not rest well down here on the stony plain,' said the pilgrim. 'He would like his mortal remains to lie on a high hill across the valley where he can overlook and protect all his beloved people.'

" 'Why, that is simple,' the people said. 'We will move his tomb there.'

"And they did. After a decent interval the British came in and built their airstrip, and the political officer began his climb to high office."

Chuckling, we both started down the hill. "The story is true, you know," said the major, "but you should also know that when I served in Miranshah I heard it told of the airstrip there, and it is also said of other airfields. What a great man that old political officer must have been!"

On the way back from Kurrum we stopped again at Thal. We planned to drive the sixty-odd miles north-east back to Kohat that day and to push on the next day an additional seventy-five miles or so south-west to Bannu. This route, which is the one prescribed by Peshawar officialdom between the two points, forms the two long sides of a narrow triangle, for Bannu is actually about 40 miles from Thal as the crow flies. There is a direct unsurfaced road which saves almost a hundred miles, but it cuts across a corner of Waziristan and is usually 'closed for repairs' because of the uncertain temperament of the Wazirs who live along it.

Mian Sahib spotted the political agent for North Waziristan among the crowds of *powendas* who were still milling about the police-station in Thal, and we all went off to share a pot of tea. Everything was peaceful in North Waziristan, the political agent said; never had it been more so. The old troublesome days had ended with the British.

"If your Wazirs are so peaceful," I said, "why do we have to drive one hundred and fifty miles through Kohat to get to Bannu?"

The political agent stroked his chin for a few moments and made a command decision. "You don't," he said. "I'm leaving in half an hour for Bannu on the direct road. You can come with me."

The political agent, we found, travelled in style. In addition to his own battered sedan he had two lorries full of *khassadars*, the irregular tribal levies who serve as a kind of personal police force for the heads of the tribal agencies. Our car was placed directly behind the political agent's. The convoy was led by one lorry and the other brought up the rear.

A mile or two outside of Thal we stopped while the Pakistani flag was broken out on the car ahead. The political agent flies the flag when he is in his own agency, just as an ambassador flies his national banner when in the country to which he is accredited. The parallel is not a bad one. In many ways the political agent is as much an ambassador as a governor. True, the agency is a part of Pakistan, but it is exempt from the national laws. The political agent represents Pakistan; his authority is great within a narrowly limited area, but if he is to succeed he must conduct his business through negotiation and conciliation rather than regulation, for in most cases he lacks the power to enforce a decision which is unacceptable to any substantial number of the tribesmen.

The countryside had already taken on a desert air. Scanning the horizon, I could not detect a single spot of green. Yet we were less than a mile from the Kurrum River. The land on both sides of the road was badly eroded by flash floods, and it was easy to see how travel would be virtually impossible during the brief rainy season.

Shortly after we began moving again, a red fox loped across the country to our right, running like a playful dog alongside the convoy. After a few hundred feet he speeded up, cut across the road in front of us, and began to pace us on the other side. That was too much for the *khassadars* in the leading lorry. The driver slammed on the brakes and a dozen whooping, shouting men piled out. The lorry behind us disgorged another dozen, and the whole crowd set out pell-mell chasing the fox who began zigzagging towards the hills a quarter of a mile away.

A young *khassadar* held out his rifle to me. After a quick glance at the political agent, who was grinning as if he had personally arranged the whole show, I grabbed the rifle and joined the pack. It was rough going and I soon lost sight of the fox as well as of the tribesman who had lent me his rifle.

There were a few shots, apparently at great distance, as the quarry made it around the shoulder of the first line of hills. A few seconds later half a dozen *khassadars* came charging back, turbans awry, full white trousers flapping wildly. They started to scramble directly up the side of the hill, hoping for a shot from the crest at the fox on the other side. One of them grabbed my hand and started to help me over the steepest places. Not satisfied with our pace, he slipped my rifle on his shoulder in addition to his own, hooked his arm in mine, and almost literally carried me up the hill at a breakneck speed. We arrived at the top just in time to see a red brush disappear behind a second line of hills.

Mian Sahib and the political agent were sitting in the shade of one of the lorries when I stumbled back, dusty and footsore. "Now you are probably the only American who can say he was on a *gusht* (patrol) with the *khassadars* in Waziristan," said the political agent. "You can even say it was a typical action."

Farther down the road we began to spot clusters of fortified houses set back a hundred yards or so from the road. Many of them were connected to the road by long, man-high ditches. Occasionally, tribesmen popped up on to the road from these ditches to wave and show their respect for the political agent as we went by.

"What are the ditches for?" I asked.

"That is very interesting," said Mian Sahib. "There used to be many very bitter blood feuds in this area. Practically every family had a feud with its neighbours. So people had to use the ditches to protect them when they left their houses to go up on the road where the government law runs and their enemies would be less willing to shoot them. All of this has died out now, of course," he added.

"If it has, why do they still use the ditches instead of just walking over the open ground?" I asked.

"It's not quite that simple," Mian Sahib explained. "They don't ordinarily shoot at each other from their houses any more, but if a man were to take to walking boldly in front of his place, his neighbour might feel that he held his fellows in low esteem. In that case honour would require that he be shot at—if only to remind him of his manners."

XI

The Warrior Bard

ISLAM LOOKS with disfavour on the graphic representation of the human figure. The message of the Holy Prophet also contains dietary restrictions and prohibits the use of alcoholic beverages. This puritanism has traditionally hindered the development of art and the refinements of living. In fact, according to one cynic, it has left no legitimate outlets for the gratification of man's senses other than 'women and the baths'

The Pathans consider their women very much their own business, and I do not care to risk claiming to know much about the subject. As for baths, much as the Pathans might like to soak or sport in scented luxury, they have little opportunity. There is scarcely enough water in the frontier hills to take care of ordinary thirst and minimal cleanliness.

The meagreness of Pathan accomplishment in the visual arts is evident in the Peshawar Museum. Amongst all the glorious sculpture there is no work which owes its creation to Pathan hands. The exquisite miniature paintings bear Mogul and Persian signatures. Even the fanciful wooden grave images are the work of the *Kafirs* of Chitral.

Yet in one field of intellectual achievement the Pathans need not take a back seat to any people in the World. They have bred poets as copiously as they have bred warriors, and often the one has been identical with the other. The memory of these poets is very much alive amongst the Pathans; their descendants, disciples, and imitators are held in high regard. It is easy to overlook this, for the outsider does not expect to find great literary figures amongst a nation of largely illiterate warrior tribesmen. In addition, few translations from the Pushtu are available and those that can be had are far from good. Yet to ignore the great literary heritage of the Pathans and the deep poetic feeling which still exists amongst them is to miss an important part of their character.

Poetry has flourished amongst the Pathans for at least three hundred years. Practically every tribe has produced a major figure of poetry at one time or another. Two of the greatest of the classic line were Mohmands: Rahman Baba and Abdul Hamid. Another was a member of the Bangash tribe, Khwaja Mohammad. Another, Ahmad Shah Abdali, the founder of the modern state of Afghanistan, was a Durrani. Known in history chiefly for his bloody raids on India, Kashmir and Persia, Ahmad Shah in his poems reveals a tortured spirit seeking God's forgiveness for his sins. In a touching couplet which suffers badly in translation, he pleads:

> May God annihilate thee, fly that is human nature!
> No mouth is uncorrupted by your impure kiss.

From a Westerner's point of view, the most interesting of the Pathan poets is Khushal Khan Khattak who, with his descendants, carried on for four generations a literary tradition which compared favourably with that of the Western world of the time.

The Khattaks are the only major tribe which has dwelled for centuries entirely in the settled districts of the Frontier. They are a clean, sturdy, attractive lot, combining, in the view of many old British administrators, most of the virtues and few of the vices of their fellow Pathans. They live along the west bank of the Indus River from Attock down to Kalabagh and have always been in closer contact with developments in the world beyond the Frontier than most of their neighbours.

The Khattaks have long been known for their relative urbanity and sophistication and their preoccupation with words. An example appears in the story of how they got their name. The tale is in the *Tarikh-i-Murassa*, a history written by Khushal Khan's grandson, Afzal Khan, in 1690. In rough translation it goes like this:

"Four Pathan brothers, Lukman, Usman, Utman and Jadran, were hunting together when they came upon four veiled girls. Usman, Utman and Jadran wanted to cast lots for the girls but Lukman insisted that, because he was the eldest, he be given first choice. He chose the girl in the finest clothes. When the others had made their selections and the veils were removed, Lukman's choice proved to be very ugly while the other three were sweet and fair. The younger brothers jeered, 'Lukman has got into the *khata* (mud),' and the name stuck to his descendants."

Khushal Khan Khattak was born in 1613, a son of the chieftain of his tribe. He was twenty-seven years old when his father fell in battle with the Yusufzai and Khushal Khan succeeded him as head of the Khattaks. Some twenty years later Khushal Khan earned the disfavour of the new Mogul emperor Aurangzeb and was imprisoned for several years in the imperial prison of Gwalior in Central India. After his release he returned home and organised a tribal confederacy against the emperor. Through bribery and promises Aurangzeb broke up the confederacy, all of the tribes except the Afridis deserting Khushal Khan. Even Khushal's own son, Bahrem, defected to the Moguls and several times sought to kill his father. Eventually Khushal Khan resigned the chieftaincy of the Khattaks to a loyal son, Ashraf—himself a noted poet—and with a small band of followers wandered from place to place in the hills pursued by the relentless Bahrem.

Khushal Khan's poems cover a wide variety of subjects. His later works, after his imprisonment and betrayal by his son and allies, have an undercurrent of bitterness and nostalgia. But even in his old age he could write glowingly of the pleasures of good hunting, fine food and beautiful women.

It is hard to convey the beauty and power of these poems. Pushtu is a highly developed language with fine nuances. The scanty English translations that have been done are mostly in the pretentious language of the Victorians. Unfortunately, I lack the ability in both English and Pushtu to attempt a completely new approach. What follows has been put together on a catch-as-catch-can basis, and I ask that the excerpts be read with a mind to their ideas and imagery rather than their words.

Khushal Khan's awareness of the beauties of nature and his love of gardens are typical of the Pathan character. So too are the martial metaphors and similes he employs in describing the delights of the World he saw around him. In recounting an interlude in a favourite garden, he says:

The stream meanders gently through the grass;
Pearls float in the fountain's froth;
The thunder of the heavens is in the waterfall.
Wild birds dive above the placid pond;
The tulips are bright as flashes from the huntsmen's guns.
The roses stand, a warrior phalanx, spears by their sides.

The seasons on the Frontier are not as we know them in Europe and North America. It is autumn, not spring, which brings coolness and new life to man and beast and sets the blood to coursing again. Three hundred years ago Khushal Khan sang thus of the coming of winter:

When Libra travels from the Sun, then does winter come.
The World, once weak with summer's heat, grows strong
   again;
Man eats with joy and finds the taste of water sweet;
Lovers embrace again, arms and lips entwined.
The warrior welcomes now his coat; the horse, his winter
   trappings;
The one feels not his armour; nor the other his saddle's
   weight.
From Swat the falcon now returns, like travelled yogi
   coming home;
And in the radiant moonlight hours comes the heron
   screaming in the sky.

The works of most of the other Pathan poets are deeply tinged with *Sufi* mysticism; they speak of physical beauty only as a symbol of metaphysical goodness. Not so of Khushal Khan. He was the father of fifty-seven sons and uncounted daughters. One can no more question the flesh and blood character of his many 'beloveds' than one can doubt the authenticity of Omar's love for the 'vintner's stuff'. Indeed, the very variety of Khushal Khan's attitudes toward women is positive proof of the reality of his interest in them. In a line of classic simplicity, he says: "Looking at the beauty of fair women, I have found my God."

Yet another poem is devoted entirely to a denunciation:

Be straightforward and honest with women;
They will be deceitful and wayward with you.

Give them a thousand gifts and caresses;
They will sulk at one untoward word.

Seek balm from their sweetness;
They will poison your life.

Although they resemble man,
They lack humanity.

They hold you wrong for the smallest offence;
Themselves guiltless of the greatest sin.

Be forbearing, they are petulant;
Humour them, they grow capricious.

Soft and beautiful on the outside,
They are venomous serpents within.

Speak of them no more, Khushal Khan;
It would be better if they had never been.

Perhaps Khushal Khan's bitterness on this occasion may have been the result, like that of the prince in the fairytale, of a single defeat amidst many conquests. At any rate, he did not give up the chase, even through all the long years of flight and futile battle against the Moguls. As the Afridis were Khushal Khan's favourites as warriors, so too did their women find favour in his eyes. He sang their praises in a rollicking verse full of the same spirit that the Tudor balladeers brought to merrie England:

Pink and white are the Adam Khel Afridi maids;
Many and varied the charms that are theirs:
Soft eyes, long lashes, and dark brows,
Sweet lips, blushing cheeks, smooth foreheads;
Their mouths are tiny rosebuds; their teeth small pearls;
Their dark tresses are fragrant amber; their skins fair, smooth
    ivory;
Their proud bodies are erect as the letter *Alif.*
Like the hawk I have flown long on the mountains,
And many a plump young partridge have I taken.
Like the hawk, whether young or old, I have sought my
    quarry,
But the swoop of the old hawk is surer and more unerring.

The ideas expressed in Khushal Khan's glorification of women in his love-poems (as many of his works clearly are) are rare in Pushtu literature, for most Pathans are far more restrained and reticent in this delicate field than their great poet. On the subjects of honour and war, however, no such distinction need be made. The old men talking over their teacups of an incident in Waziristan in 1936 or the raid on Peshawar in 1930 evoke with their words graphic images which rival Khushal Khan's own.

War and honour are the proper business of the Pathan, be he farmer, trader, or poet, and it is while speaking of these that Khushal Khan is at his best. "The young men have dyed red their hands," he says, "like the falcon dyes his talons in the blood of his prey. They have ruddied their pale swords with gore: they have made the tulip-bed blossom in the middle of the summer."

They have reddened the Khyber with the blood of the foe;
They have made the mountains of Bajaur quake and tremble
    with their cannon;
For five long years, every day has seen the flashing of their
    swords.
We fought with Mir Hussein in the Doab, and crushed his
    head as we would a snake;
After that we fought at Naoshera, until I became drunk with
    Mogul blood.
We have scattered the treasures of India before us;
We have given back to the mountains Aurangzeb's red gold;
Between him and us there can be no bargaining,
The Moguls or the Pathans will be destroyed.

Glorifying the fighting powers of the Khattaks and the leadership of his loyal son, Abad, Khushal Khan sings in part of a long epic:

Abad Khan came home from battle,
Welcome was the gift he brought.
Although his robes were cut to tatters, and
His face poppy red with blood,
Victory smiled on Abad Khan.
He has honoured his father's name.
God grant he rival him in fame and deed;
His hand be ever victorious.
Let his sword drink blood like a dragon.
Khattak spears pierce the chain armour,
Like the tailor needles the cloth of the tent.
Khattak lancers ride over the Bangash,

And shatter them root and branch.
Plunder is ours: lovely maidens, fine horses,
  and precious jewels.
All our men bear the black armour, the quills,
  and the bows of the foe.

Khushal Khan's interests, however, went beyond the ordinary
warrior's love of plunder and joy of battle. His diplomatic dealings with the Moguls and his constant negotiation to create a
grand alliance of the Pathan tribes showed great skill in statecraft.
He put some of this knowledge down in lyrical little aphorisms,
such as one demonstrating the faults and weaknesses of different
classes of which a ruler might take advantage: 'Violence for kings;
roguery for priests; parsimony for rich men; luxury for women.'
  A short poem on the character of a monarch is simple, yet
comprehensive:

> He who fears to risk his life,
> Or who grudges money spent,
> Never will be chief or monarch,
> Nor will conquered lands be his.
> The throne or the bier,
> Are the only resting-places of kings.

Khushal Khan set down his advice to rulers in a classic piece
which rivals anything that Dante or Machiavelli had to say.
Robbed of literary beauty in translation, the hard facts of king-
ship are still made clear:

Until the sovereign has cut off many heads,
The plains and mountains of the land will not be still.
Either others will mourn at your door for your death,
Or they must weep for those slaughtered at your hand.
He that finds fault with your rule,
Be quit of him, by gold, by treachery, or by arms.
Whatever you may do by the sword, the arrow, or the lance,
A hundred-fold more is gained by skill and strategy.
Slay your son and your brother for the security of your state;
Closely guard your rivals in your jails.
Only the water of the sword can quench

The fevered thirst of him who yearns for war.
The tree of a chief's sovereignty, well watered
By the blood of his enemies, bears fair fruit.
It is better that bleeding heads should lie on the battlefield,
Than that live hearts should carry evil blood.
Either like a man enfold the turban on your head,
Or wear in its place a woman's veil.
Oh God! What use my writing? Who will heed me?
Yet have I said what must be said.

Khushal Khan's harshness probably resulted in no small part from the difficulties he encountered in trying to organise and promote the welfare of his own people. The tribes were vigorous and independent and little inclined to submit themselves to Khushal Khan's direction. The Moguls took advantage of this; one Mogul governor succeeded in breaking up an alliance by getting one of the tribes to demand an agreement on a division of the spoils before a battle was fought. All in all, Khushal Khan spent more time in fighting his fellow tribesmen than the Moguls. In one little verse, he comments bitterly:

All Pathans are evilly-disposed;
From house to house they fighting go.
Let one but lift his head a bit;
Another quickly lays him low.

Again he says:

The Pathans lack sense and understanding:
They are tail-cut curs of the slaughter-house.
They play away dominion for Mogul gold;
They lust after offices that the Moguls give.
Though the camel with its rich load comes into their house,
They are first taken up with stealing the bell from its neck.
A curse upon him who first bore the name,
And maledictions upon all that follow after.
They begin at Kandahar and reach unto Damghar,
And all are worthless who dwell between.

In another damning litany, Khushal Khan grants a saving grace at the very end:

If the Pathan folk are of the human race at all,
In manners and ways they are very Hindus.
They have neither skill nor wisdom,
But are happy in ignorance and strife.
They obey neither the law of their fathers,
Nor the instructions of their teachers.
Whenever one worthy man rises amongst them,
They all seek his life.
They never forget to injure one another;
Hence calamity always remembers them.
They respect not themselves nor do others respect them,
Though there are more of them than locusts or ants.
Now I, then others, as many as may be,
Require aid or a helping hand;
But whether it is courage or generosity that may be asked,
They will through quarrelling throw both away.
But still, O Khushal Khan, thank God for this;
That they are not slaves, but free-born men!

Like many another poet and king, Khushal Khan eventually
became impressed with the emptiness of this World and the
futility of its strivings. What he has to say could have come from
the pen of a medieval saint of Europe. It contrasts starkly with
the joy of life which surges through most of his works:

There will be none of this World's vanities and ambitions
within the tomb:
Man's own good deeds will go with him, and naught else
besides.
Without the parrot, the cage is nothing: know you this!
And the soul is like unto the parrot, the body like unto the
cage.
Be careful that it may not be altogether lost,
For a most precious thing is this soul of yours.
Whoever casts this sacred gem unprofitably away,
Like unto the dumb brutes of the fields is he.
Pass near the graves of chiefs and nobles of this land;
Behold, out of their dust have thorns and brambles come.
Whatever will be, will be; why then this apprehension and
this dread?

It is our lot from the World to take at most a shroud away,
And that too will be but eight or nine yards long, or maybe
     ten.
Pretty maids, noble steeds, brocaded robes,
All these will remain behind me here.
Prepare, O Khushal, for the time is come—
All around me is the sound of the warning bell.

One thing, however, Khushal Khan valued to the end: honour.
His poems, early and late, sad and joyous, are full of it. "Though
my enemy rejoices over me for a while," he says, "those who die
are not the only warriors I have. They are but a few guests whom
I invited to sup in honour's cause."

> Sweeter to me is death than that life,
> Which is passed day to day without honour.
> Though he will not live forever in this world,
> Yet the memory of Khushal Khan will abide.

In the seventy-eighth year of his life, the old chieftain died as
he had lived, fearless and free. He was buried in the Khattak
Mountains in an isolated spot where, in his own words, "the dust
of the hooves of the Mogul cavalry may not light on my grave".
The tomb remains today, not far from Akora.

True to his Pathan honour, Khushal Khan left instructions that
if any of his loyal sons should succeed in getting their hands upon
their traitorous brother, Bahrem, they should bring him to his
father's grave, cut him in two, and burn one part of him at the
head and the other at the foot of the dead chief's grave.

XII

The Great Migration

THE AUTUMN brings excitement to the Frontier. As Khushal
Khan said: "The World, once weak with summer's heat,
grows strong again." The annual migration of the *powendas*,
from the highlands of Afghanistan down to the Indus Plain, is
one of the most impressive sights of this strong, new world. Less
well known than the seasonal migrations of the southern Iranian
tribes and the Arab bedouin, the trek of the *powendas* is almost
certainly the greatest remaining mass movement of men and
animals in a world in which man's most persistent tendency for
half a dozen millennia has been to settle down.

The *powendas*, or *kūchis* as they are known in Afghanistan,
cross the Border through the Khyber, the Kurrum, the Tochi,
the Gomal, and by a hundred lesser-known routes. They spread
out all over the Frontier and beyond into Sind and the Punjab.
In the spring they return to Afghanistan, penetrating into and
beyond the high central plateau, the Hazarajat. The movement
takes place every year and involves 100,000 to 300,000 people.

Powenda, as used on the Frontier, means simply 'nomad'. Most
of the nomads are Pathans and nearly all of them speak Pushtu.
They belong to the Ghilzai branch of the Pathans whose historic
home is around Kandahar and the Ghazni Plain in Afghanistan.
There are many individual tribes within the Ghilzai group, the
Aka Khel, the Ali Khel, the Suleiman Khel, and a score of others.

There is no uniformity and little apparent organisation of the
migration. Sometimes whole villages move as a unit, driving
their flocks before them to set up camp on the eastern skirts of
the Border Hills. Other groups consist of men who have deposited their families somewhere *en route* and bring down goods
to trade in Pakistan. At one time the *powendas* were important
carriers in the caravan trade between Central Asia and India.
Their imports are now limited to crudely tanned hides and skins
and roughly hewn timber.

Some groups are evidently prosperous and travel with all the
luxury of Central Asian caravans: flocks of camels and sheep,
furniture, servants, and liberal food stocks. Others are miserably
poor, and come to offer themselves for the hardest agricultural
labour in return for water and fodder for their few animals.
Some have no animals at all and trudge along living off the
countryside as best they can. A few are money-lenders, traditionally but incorrectly known as 'Kabulis' amongst the villagers
of Sind and the Punjab where their transactions involve only
a few rupees in capital but bring in a profit of several hundred
per cent.

I set out one autumn to observe the *powendas* on their inexorable
march. I saw them first in late October along the road east of
Kabul in Afghanistan. Their pace was leisurely. They marched
a few hours in the early morning and camped for the rest of
the day. Little eddies of them, a single family or perhaps two,
drifted down the narrow·valleys to the north and the south of
the road. Once beside the high road to the Khyber they lingered,
some days not breaking camp at all, moving no more than a
dozen miles in a week. Their children and their unveiled women
moved about searching for a few sticks for the family fire or
carrying a smoke-blackened copper pot of water from some
distant well.

The men were seldom to be seen. Some were still in the highlands where they had tarried to collect their flocks or to cut a
last rough timber balk to bring down for sale in Pakistan. Others
earned forage for their animals or access to a well by menial
tasks for the Afghan farmers of the valleys. A few were already
across the Frontier negotiating with the landlords of the Peshawar
Valley for the labour of their people in the following winter.

The roadside camps were unimpressive: ragged, black tents
hung insecurely on shaky sticks, the dark smears of dead fires
scarring the ground around them. Animals were few and mangy:
an aged camel, a few goats, a sheep or two. Except for the
bright-faced babies swaddled in rags, the children were lethargic
and dull-eyed. Their mothers and grandmothers, all looking
three score years and ten, squatted by the tents, moving only to
set another copper pot on the fire or to draw a corner of their
black rags across seamed and grimy faces when I approached. No
camp of gypsies in medieval Europe ever looked so poor. It was

not difficult to understand the note of contempt which sounded in the voices of the local Afghans when they spoke of the *kūchis*, and they urged me to show them no mercy while driving through their scattered ranks on the road.

A week later, when I drove from Kabul to Peshawar, there were signs that the aimless movement which stirred sluggishly in the trough of the Kabul River Valley was beginning to take on some purpose and sense of direction. The squalid camps by the roadside were still there, but as our Jeep climbed laboriously up and around the hairpin turns of the Lataband Pass, through which runs the Kabul-Jelalabad road, we passed innumerable small caravans.

The camels were under control here. Tall, black-turbaned ruddy-bearded men led them along at a fast walk, swinging the whole string from one side of the road to the other with great skill to make way for the Jeep. Laughing boys ran in and out between the camels' legs. A wave and a shouted 'thank you' brought a flash of white teeth and a wide grin in return. The creak of harness and the slap-slap of feet and hooves bespoke vigour and purpose.

In almost every string of camels there was one with a small child perched on top of a mountain of baskets and tents. Head bobbing in rhythm with the plodding of the camel, the small round face looked solemnly out on the world from beneath a gaily embroidered pillar-box hat. Sometimes a necklace of silver coins or a pair of startlingly large ear-rings would indicate that the mite was a girl. Nearly always the little creatures looked happy, healthy, and at ease.

'Brides' camels' with their precious loads were almost as common as those with babies. The harness of the beast was usually new and rich, the blankets, which made up the load, cleaner and more colourful than those of the others. Mischievous, shining eyes peered over a black robe, casually held in hands red with henna and shining with silver rings and bangles. Dark eyes, fixed on the back of lord and master plodding at the head of the caravan, were quick to turn their gaze on the passing stranger. Occasionally the robe dropped altogether, to give a glimpse of a face such as that which captured the unknown king by the Kurrum stream so long ago.

In quick succession, we passed half a dozen of these flashes of unexpected beauty. My eye caught that of the Afghan Jeep driver who obviously was giving the 'brides' camels' as close a scrutiny as was I. "Where do all these beautiful girls come from?" I asked. "There were none in the camps down there by the road."

"*Kūchi* women no good," he said, "let any man see them."

"We didn't see any like these back towards Kabul," I said.

"Man has fine young wife," he explained, "he keeps her with him all the time. He doesn't send her to wait with old women by the road."

We drove in silence for a few minutes while he negotiated the vehicle up a particularly steep hairpin just below the crest of the pass. As we came out on the top, we drew abreast of another caravan. A husky, moustachioed young man wearing a blue waist-coat embroidered with silver led the string of camels, most of them loaded with timbers. A boy of ten or twelve, probably his younger brother, walked beside him. They were talking earnestly. The second beast in the line carried the trappings of a bride. At the top of it sat a striking girl of the type Hollywood puts in romantic gipsy films. She sat erect, disdaining any pretension of the veil, silver flashing from her ears, bodices, and wrists. Beyond her, across miles and miles of hazy blue air, were the black and white peaks of the Hindu Kush.

I held my breath in admiration. The driver grunted. "Next year, maybe she wait by the side of the road too," he said with a touch of malice.

"Well, there was certainly nothing like her there this year," I countered.

"Next year maybe she not look like that. She look like those others you see back there," he said.

Unfortunately, he was telling the truth. From Peshawar I moved on up to Swat where the first of the *powenda* caravans to enter Pakistan were trickling down through the obscure little northern passes which run eastwards from the Kunar River Valley. There were beautiful brides here too, but they were few amongst the total women of the families and clans which had united and were moving eastwards. The life of the road takes a harsh toll of the *powenda* women. Fair skin, smooth hair, and sleek bodies come quickly at fifteen or sixteen and are gone within a few years. The old hags by the side of the Kabul Road were the brides of a few seasons past. Those who looked seventy were yet to see forty; they were remarkable amongst their kind, less that they had once been beautiful, than that they had lived so long.

It is otherwise with the men. Like others from the Aran Islands to the Mongolian steppes who live and toil in the open, they grow handsomer and more stately as the years and the elements beat down on them.

One sturdy chieftain led his caravan down the road above Saidu Sharif in Swat. He strode along in boat-shaped slippers decorated in silver and gold with soles two inches thick. The stains on his white pantaloons had been blanched by the dust of the road. A long, royal purple shirt hugged his ribs, its ends flapping against his calves like a bishop's chasuble. A splendid sheep-skin waistcoat, wool side in and brilliant yellow outside, hung open on his chest. A silver amulet nestled on the bronzed vee where his shirt opened at the throat. Grey eyes sparkled beneath a black turban. His great hawk nose hung over a spreading moustache and bushy beard as ruddy as his cheeks.

This magnificent figure did not deign to lead his own camels. He marched in front, shouting a hoarse cadence and keeping time with a polished wooden staff. Younger editions of himself led the three strings of camels and kept herd on a group of fat-tailed sheep who brought up the rear. All of them had the unmistakable features and robust physiques of their sire.

He stopped to talk. Camels, sheep, and men piled up around us, children and women peering down between the boxes and bales that hung on the heaving humps. To my surprise, he broke immediately into familiar English. "You camp with me tonight, Sahib, and I kill a sheep for us, eh?" he asked. "I've been all over," he explained, "to Calcutta, Delhi, Bombay. I know many talks, all good."

I was less interested in Calcutta, Delhi and Bombay than in where he was now coming from. The tangled knot of the Pamirs, where Pakistan, Afghanistan, the USSR and China come together, was less than a hundred miles at his back. He looked as if he had walked twice that distance in the past fortnight.

He either could not or would not tell me. With a quick glance at the Pakistani political official who sat in our car benignly observing the conversation, the *powenda* waved his staff vaguely in the directions of north and west. "Over the mountains that way—not far, Sahib," he said. "Same every year; me and my people come here to work in winter. We will tell police at Malakand we come. Everything is all right."

"Badakhshan? Nuristan?" I inquired. These are the Afghan provinces adjacent to the Border on the north-west.

"Yes, Sahib, that right. You have been these places?"

I tried again. "Wakhan, maybe?" Wakhan is the narrow tongue of Afghanistan which touches China and divides Pakistan from the Soviet Union.

"Yes, Sahib, there too. Very nice place."

I thanked him for his offer of hospitality, which I could not accept, and prepared to leave. "Wait minute, Sahib," he said, "maybe you like know. Up there, where you say," he gestured back at the mountains, "I see men, strange men, uniforms with stars, guns, radios, many machines, lot of horses. They come this way, not on road. Bad men, I think, Russians, I think."

I felt like Kipling confronted with Mahbub Ali whispering of "a grey-coat guard on the Helmund ford". I began to try to phrase questions to pry out this nugget of intelligence. Before I could speak, my Pakistani guide slipped into the circle and took over the interrogation. In a casual voice, he asked half a dozen questions in a mixture of Pushtu and English. A few of the younger men added details to their leader's account. After a few minutes we all shook hands and in a shower of benedictions went our separate ways.

Back in the car, I asked, "Shouldn't we tell someone right away? I didn't get it all but it sounded important."

"Let's wait a little and see," he replied.

After eight or ten miles, our car swung down into a detour along the riverbed to avoid a section of the road which was being repaired by a road-gang under the direction of a couple of Pakistani Army surveyors. The political officer pointed. "There are your men, uniforms, and machines," he said with a grin.

The description tallied exactly. "Did the *powenda* know?" I asked.

He shrugged. "Maybe, maybe not. He would probably say it was all the same to him anyway."

The migratory stream swelled even during the few days I spent in Swat. The Malakand Pass was choked with *powenda* caravans when we came down through it, and every clearing along the canals of Mardan District was cluttered with their camps.

I stopped to see my Mohmand friends near Takht-i-Bhai and found them directing groups of *powendas* to clean the canals and drainage ditches which run between their cane-fields. *Powenda* children gleaned the harvested fields, picking up dried and broken cane for fuel and forage and occasionally finding a stalk with some juice left in it to suck. The women were setting up their ragged tents and, although they had arrived only that morning, the campsite already had a look of permanency about it.

By late November Peshawar was bustling with the ingress of nomads. The stirrings which I had observed a month earlier beyond the Lataband had grown into a full flood pouring through the passes and out on to the Pakistani plain. In the Peshawar Bazaar the soft slurred Pushtu spoken by most of the *powendas* swelled above the guttural northern Pukhtu which usually prevailed there. The cobblers and the tea-shops did a thriving trade. *Powenda* families trooped through the central square, the Chowk Yad Gar, drinking in the sights of the metropolis as avidly as any Western tourist. A few, with their camels, even managed to penetrate the staid cantonment, despite the frantic efforts of the local traffic police to direct them around it.

The road between Peshawar and the Khyber was flanked on both sides by virtually continuous lines of people and animals trudging eastwards. Counting roughly by tens, I drove past more than a thousand nomads in the few minutes it took to reach Peshawar University from the cantonment airfield.

The old administration building of the university is close by the road, and I stopped to sit on the steps and watch the caravans move by. Across the way lay the green lawns and snow-white minarets of the university mosque. In front of them passed a living frieze of a world which we in the West have never known. The brown and grey shapes passing by were stark and timeless: a string of camels, humps swaying, heads to tails; flocks of sheep and goats in scurrying clumps; a tiny swaddled figure on top of a solitary hump; a straight, high-breasted girl striding along with a copper water-vessel on her head; a bearded patriarch leaning on his staff. The moving bands of figures seemed to represent permanence and reality while the lawns and towers were a transitory backdrop.

A couple of students from the college had joined me on the steps when I first sat down and we had talked of examinations and jobs. As my imagination had been seized by the moving figures, I had forgotten my companions and we ceased to speak. When I finally broke the spell and rose to leave, I noticed that the drama by the road had transfixed one of the boys beside me also. He got to his feet slowly, still looking at the passing caravans, and, without any attempt to explain further, said, "My grand-father came that way."

Fort Jamrud, at the entrance to the Khyber, swarmed with *powendas*, many of them looking jealously at the Enfield rifles carried by the local Afridis and prowling eagerly about in the small gun-factories in Jamrud village. Farther up the pass lines of women stood to draw water at the spring near Ali Masjid, running to catch up with their caravans when their vessels were full. The little plain beyond Torkhum at the Afghan Border was dark with the nomads. The only formality required for their Border crossing seemed to be that they thinned down into single-file between groups of Pakistani officials as they stepped across the line.

I found similar scenes being enacted two hundred miles farther south along the Frontier. Only an occasional small caravan was in evidence as I drove down the main north-south road which runs parallel to the border between Peshawar and Baluchistan. However, where the main highway was crossed by a lateral road coming down from the passes, the nomad stream swept by. The flow down the Kurrum enveloped Kohat. The outpourings of the Tochi seethed around Bannu. The traffic through the Gomal spread out into Tank, Kulachi, and Dera Ismail Khan. In Baluchi-stan, still farther south, Fort Sandeman, Quetta, and Sibi absorbed and channelled the human tide. Between all of these places a hundred rivulets of humanity made their way eastwards through little cracks in the Border Hills which never rated a name on even the most elaborate survey maps.

These patterns of movement have long had a significance far greater than that of a seasonal migration. They are the very core of 'the strategy of the Frontier', a subject dear to the heart of anyone who has ever spent more than a few days in the land of the Pathans. Frontier strategy is still pertinent, even in an age of nuclear weapons, and it is worth while to take a few moments to consider it.

First, look at the map; imagine the topography. A virtually

impenetrable mass of mountains—the Himalayas linking on to Pamirs, Pamirs on to Hindu Kush—runs across the top, separating South Asia from the Soviet Union and China. Then another range, the Suleiman Mountains, runs down the Pakistani-Afghan border until it peters out in the sterile wastes of eastern Persia and Baluchistan. The key factor to remember is that this range is not impassable. The Khyber is not the only pass through it. It is merely the most convenient and the best known.

The natural flow of peoples in this area has always been west-east through the Suleiman passes. The Persians, the Greeks, the Afghans, and the Moguls all came through the passes. Those Pathans who now live in Pakistan came this way. The roads they trod still remain in a large degree the rutted tracks they have been through the ages, though the British extended paved highways up some of the important arteries, notably Kurrum and the Khyber, in order to bring up their troops more efficiently to oppose invasion. Between the arteries, the hills and the little un-marked passes are, as they have always been, the exclusive pre-serve of the Pathans.

What the British did was to build north-south roads parallel to the mountains. On these they could intercept and regulate the flow coming down, and in a day or two rush a battalion from its position in Peshawar maintaining a defence of the Khyber to a position in Tank defending the Gomal. The improvements made in the east-west roads running up the passes enabled them to push out rapidly to meet the enemy at or beyond the crest. It is over these east-west roads to and through the passes that the Pathans maintain their power today. An invader coming down into Pakistan or a defender going up to hold the passes is equally at the mercy of the tribesmen who occupy the hills on both sides of the line of march. This, in its simplest and most elementary form, is the 'strategy of the Frontier'.

But let us go back to the *powendas*. Returning from South Waziristan to Peshawar, I turned aside at Bannu to go up the Tochi Valley to watch the caravans coming down. A political officer and a squad of *khassadars*, the agency levies, came with me, for there had been rumours of clashes between the *powendas* and the resident Wazir and Mahsud tribes farther down the Border.

A little beyond Miranshah I stopped to photograph a caravan of the nomads. At this point the road constitutes the dividing line between the territory of the Wazir and the Daur tribes. The Wazirs are amongst the most fierce of all the Pathan tribes. The Daurs are known among their fellow Pathans (unjustly, as far as I can see) as particularly treacherous and vice-ridden. There is also a tendency among the other tribes to consider their very Pathanishness as in some way questionable and to attribute their character to bad, that is, non-Pathan, bloodlines.

While I was focusing my camera on the *powendas*, a little knot of Daurs gathered on one side of the road. A party of Wazirs drifted up to stand opposite on the other side. One of the latter could not pass up the opportunity for delivering a taunt. Assuming that the stranger in Western dress was English, he pointed and shouted, "Hey, Daurs, your grandfather has come back."

The insult stung; the Daurs moved out on the road, knives in hand. Several *khassadars* dashed between the would-be combatants and shoved them back off the road. One of them explained, "This is not an Englishman. He is an American. He is nobody's grandfather."

Heading back for Bannu, we stopped briefly to see the Kurrum Garhi project, which is one of Pakistan's major efforts to develop the Frontier. Masses of tribesmen swarmed over the huge earthfill dam, the heart of the scheme.

A young Pakistani engineer described the project to us in enthusiastic terms. It would, he emphasised, ensure dependable irrigation for 130,000 acres already under cultivation and provide water for another 150,000 acres now lying barren. "We will settle the tribesmen on this land and other land like it," he said, "and we will solve a problem the British were never able to do."

A *powenda* family was camped near where we stood. A ragged lad of about fourteen brought us over a handful of fresh sugarcane and stayed to listen to the strange English words and observe the men in foreign dress.

"Do the tribes want to settle on the land?" I asked the engineer.

"Of course, why not? They have nothing now," he answered.

Nothing except a way of life which did not go with following a plough, I reflected. Unconvinced, I said, "Ask this boy here if he would like to own some of the new land and farm it."

The engineer was reluctant. "He is just a boy," he said. "He has never known anything but trekking along the road."

"Let's just see what he says," I persisted.

"He is not one of our tribesmen. He comes from Afghanistan. Besides, he might think I was offering him the land and then there would be trouble." The engineer evaded the question.

"O, come on," I said. "He looks very bright and he knows we are talking about him now."

The prophet of development gave up. "I don't speak Pushtu," he finally admitted.

The political officer squatted down and began to speak softly to the boy in Pushtu. He told him about the dam and the new land. He asked him if he would like to own some of it, to live in a new house, to give up his camels, to farm the land, to obey the laws, and to live always in one place.

The boy was silent for so long that we thought he had not understood. Then, he said simply, "Yes."

The political officer sensed that I had not got the answer I expected. On the way back, he explained. "It is interesting that the boy should say 'yes'. A few years ago that would never have happened. Even now, his father would not say 'yes', and perhaps when the boy is grown and leads his own caravan, he will not say so either. If he did settle on the land he might not like it. The Kabul Government brought many tribesmen to new land in the Helmand Valley, but most of them did not like it and ran away. Still, the tribesmen see what is happening here, and sooner or later they will want to share in it. When they do, we will be ready."

The incident reminded me of the first time I had heard of the *powendas*. It was in Karachi some years earlier, when I was still new to the country and to the complexities of Frontier life.

I was sitting after dinner with a number of diplomats and Pathan officials, amongst them the chief minister of the North-West Frontier Province, Khan Abdul Qaiyum Khan. The topic of conversation had been the nomads: the burden their annual migration placed on the Frontier economy, the damage they did to crops, the diseases they brought, the complaints they provoked from the resident tribesmen. Extra food ration-cards had to be issued for them. Wheat had to be imported from the Punjab to feed them. Public health teams had to be diverted from their work in the villages to inoculate and delouse the *powendas* and to tend their sick. "They cost us *lakhs* [hundreds of thousands] of rupees every year," one official concluded sadly.

"Well, why don't you stop them from coming?" I asked, "or at least, don't give them anything when they do?"

The chief minister, sophisticated, Westernised, a barrister of the Inner Temple in London, answered:

"What else can we do but help them? They are our own people."[1]

---

[1] This chapter was prepared for publication before the Government of Pakistan closed the Border to the *powendas* in the winter of 1961–62. The full effect of the Border closing on the way of life of the *powendas* cannot yet be determined, but it appears likely that even now the last of the really great migrations of the World's peoples is ended.

XIII

Waziristan: the Dark and Bloody Ground

SOUTH OF THE smiling Kurrum Valley lies a five-thousand-square-mile tangle of hills with the sinister-sounding name of Waziristan. Here *Pukhtunwali* is the only way of life. Here the Pathan may be found at his cruellest—and his noblest. Here great and proud men have tasted defeat and humiliation.

The very landmarks have grown out of dark and bloody deeds: the tree under which a British political agent of long ago was murdered by his trusted orderly because the orderly took insult from his master's gift to a fellow tribesman of a rifle better than his own; the curtain-shrouded bedroom where another political agent shot himself because the government refused to honour his promises to the tribes; the Shahur Tangi, a narrow defile between Tank and Wana, where a British convoy was cut to pieces in an ambush in 1937.

Other places have their links, also dark and bloody, with broader trends of history: the airstrip at Miranshah, where Pandit Nehru, crusading for a united India, barely escaped with his life in 1946; the barracks nearby where T. E. Lawrence, the hero of Arabia, sought oblivion as an enlisted man in the Royal Air Force; the nondescript village where Amin Jan, half-brother of the deposed King Amanulla of Afghanistan and long-time pretender to the throne of Kabul, schemes and dreams as befits his royal blood.

The dress of the southern tribesmen is rougher and more sombre than that of their brothers in the North. The men wrap their black turban-cloths directly about their heads, disdaining the golden basket around which the Afridis and Mohmands wind their blue and white turbans. Trousers and shirts are dark in hue. Knives are more in evidence than rifles. The hills are more blasted and barren than in the North; the passes through them, narrower and more twisting.

The little hospital which the government maintains in

Miranshah, headquarters of the North Waziristan Agency, looks like an oasis of stability and orderliness. When I first approached it the building shone with fresh whitewash; the veranda glistened after a recent mopping. The doctor who showed me about was an urbane man who used his pipe for a pointer as he indicated the laboratory, X-ray room, operating theatre, and pharmacy.

"About average this week," he said of the surgical ward. He gestured at the half-dozen tribesmen and a young boy who occupied the beds. "Six gun-shot wounds. All 'accidental'."

As an afterthought, he added, "The lad has a broken leg from a fall—also 'accidental'."

The patients stared solemnly back at us. One, whose face and eyes were covered with bandages, said something in Pushtu and the doctor replied soothingly. "He insists on knowing who everybody who comes into the ward is," the doctor explained. "His rifle burst when he was firing at an enemy and he is afraid that the enemy will come here to kill him while he cannot see."

The hospital was behind a double wall and platoons of the Tochi Scouts had been everywhere about as I came in.

"I should think he would be safe here," I ventured.

The doctor shrugged. "Who knows? At least, he's probably safer now than he ever will be again."

Most of the men in the hospital were Wazirs, members of the largest of the southern tribes. There are about 200,000 Wazirs in all, scattered in a great arc along the Durand Line. The first Englishman who came into contact with the Wazirs early in the nineteenth century professed to find them trustworthy and likeable. Contact with 'civilisation' must have been responsible for a change in their character, however, for by the later part of the century their reputation for savage aggressiveness was well established.

The Wazirs stand convicted of one of the very few failings of the Pathans in observing the obligations of *Pukhtunwali*. The story is an old one, but it is still remembered on the Frontier, and records may be found in dusty files in London. The setting was the Maizar villages near Datta Khel in the North Waziristan Agency.

One morning in June 1897 a British political officer, one Mr Gee, came to the villages without prior warning. His purpose was to select a site for a small fort the British wanted to erect in the neighbourhood. The Wazirs did not know this and were suspicious that he intended to confiscate their lands because they had not paid a fine which had been assessed against them for killing a Hindu the previous year.

They were surprised and frightened by Gee's sudden arrival with an unusually large escort. Yet they professed to welcome him and laid out a meal for the British party. While Gee and his friends relaxed with the food and the security of the protection which the extension of *melmastia*, hospitality, always entailed, the tribesmen fell upon them and killed several officers. The killings at Maizar touched off a flame which spread all over the Frontier and culminated in the uprising of 1897, the greatest the British ever had to face.

The twentieth century brought no end to Wazir intransigence. They played a large part in the revolt which followed the Third Afghan War in 1919–1920. In 1929 they were mainly responsible for putting Nadir Shah on the Afghan throne. In their last great contest with the British in 1936 and 1937 they tied down almost 50,000 regulars of the British Indian Army in two years of guerrilla warfare.

Their land is a fitting background for these wild deeds. With the exception of small parts of the Tochi and Gomal Valleys, where a few crops and animals can survive, the grey and brown rock is unrelieved with the smallest touch of green.

Within this barren and blasted land was born and reared a wiry little man of the Tori Khel Wazirs who for the past thirty years held undisputed claim to the title of 'the Frontier's most notorious hostile'. Mirza Ali Khan was the name he carried from his birth in about 1890, but he was more widely known and feared as the Fakir of Ipi. When he died in the April of 1960 the Fakir had more than thirty years of active hostility to authority—both British and Pakistani—behind him.

The Fakir was prone to treachery and the most brutal kind of warfare. He played on the religious prejudices of the tribesmen. He took bribes from all who would pay them. He sheltered the most depraved outlaws. He offered bonuses to his followers for the kidnapping or killing of the children of the political authorities in the tribal agencies. Few who had dealings with him, especially in his later years, would argue with a Pakistani official's characterisation of him as "a vicious old man, twisted with hate and selfishness".

Yet Ipi was a legend on the Frontier long before his death, and the legend was not without a glamorous tone. His religious appeal as the arch-enemy of the alien and infidel laws and customs of the British and the Hindus accounted for much of his early success. Yet part of his appeal to the freedom-loving tribesmen lay in his independence. "He took gold from anyone but he served no one," one *malik* explained to me with grudging admiration. Another attraction was his dogged resistance to authority long after hope of victory had passed. For his last score of years he was holed up in a cliffside cave at Gorweckht, astride the Durand Line, and defied all comers. He was still there when he died, with only a few followers at his side, devoid of all the comforts and trappings of prestige which surround the successful *malik*.

Ironically, the Ipi legend was taken up at the end by his oldest and most implacable foes. His obituary ran for more than half a column in *The Times* of April 20, 1960. He was described as 'a man of principle and saintliness . . . the inspiration and general of tribal revolt . . .'

'Many retired army officers and political agents who served on the Frontier will hear the news [of his death] with the tribute of wistful regret, which is to the memory of a doughty and honourable opponent,' *The Times* concluded.

Any glistening eyes and clearing of throats which the obituary may have inspired in the London clubs must have drawn a wry chuckle from the Fakir enjoying the rewards which Paradise provides for true fighters for the faith.

In the geographic centre of Waziristan, half-way between Miranshah in the north and Wana in the south, lies the great cantonment of Razmak. The construction of Razmak in the 1920s represented the ultimate achievement of British 'Forward Policy' in dealing with the tribes. There was space for thousands of men and their supplies within the walls surrounding the cantonment. Whole regiments could be deployed and quartered there. Hard-surfaced roads, built at great cost in money and blood, radiated out through the country of the Wazirs and the Mahsuds. The Afghan Border was a scant twenty miles away.

Razmak is still marked in large letters on the maps issued by the Survey of Pakistan, and the red lines of main roads still twist out from it to the north, south, and east. Few outsiders have travelled them, however, since 1947, when the British abandoned the cantonment; the speeding convoys of armed lorries have given way to an occasional foot-weary Mahsud or Wazir. Within the cantonment itself the barracks' doors swing in the dry wind and each year the bright colours of the regimental insignia emblazoned on the walls grow a little dimmer.

Occasionally, upon the invitation of the local *maliks*, a few Pakistani officials come out for an *al fresco* lunch in the shadow of the great monument to British imperial policy. But really the cantonment has reverted to what it was before the coming of the invader.

Many stories of the brave fights which took place around Razmak linger on, however, and old soldiers, both Pukhtun and British, relish the telling of them.

There is the account of the company of Pathan militia which, under British command, was engaged in a running fight with a band of insurgent tribesmen trying to reach the safety of the Afghan Border. Every day and every night the militia banged away at their tribal brothers with great noise and enthusiasm and the tribesmen banged back. There were few casualties on either side and every twenty-four hours the fighting moved closer to the Border. The British officer in command of the operation was counting on his foes exhausting their ammunition, at which time he planned to overrun and capture or disperse them and have done with the campaign.

When after several days the nightly fire continued as heavily as ever, he began to wonder about the supplies of the enemy— not to speak of the sincerity of his own warriors. He secretly instructed his sergeant-major to issue tracer bullets in the morning's ammunition distribution to the *khassadars* (militia). When darkness fell, he had his answer. The regular drumfire of shooting began from the surrounding hills but now each shot was a long streak of light, carefully directed away from the tents of the sleeping *khassadars*.

There was also the ancient matter of civil versus military control over operations on the Frontier. When trouble was brewing, the civilian political agent tried to forestall it by mediation, negotiation, or outright bribery. If after a certain number of days he had not been successful, Government moved in far-away Calcutta or

New Delhi and the military took charge. A column of troops was mounted and moved out against the offending tribe. The political agent almost invariably opposed this, but his job required him to go along as a subordinate adviser to the military commander. He was usually viewed with considerable scorn by the stout soldiers whose recipe for handling troublesome tribesmen was inevitably 'a whiff of gunpowder'.

There is a much-told story of one such occasion when the punitive column had been harassed by daily skirmishes with the tribesmen, who seemed able to anticipate every move and intention of the soldiers. The harried colonel was grateful that he saw little of the political agent, who rose early and disappeared from sight until the nightly staff conference in the colonel's tent.

One evening after the firing had been particularly heavy, the colonel was receiving casualty reports from his company commanders: "Three, five, two, and eleven . . . that makes twenty-one more today," he summed up grumpily.

Just then, the political agent slipped into the tent; sweating and puffing, he brushed the dust of the hills from his jacket. "Twenty-one," he repeated brightly. "Why that's capital! My chaps lost only three."

A dozen or so miles south of the silent cantonment at Razmak lies a capital of another sort: Kanigurum, the chief place of the Mahsuds, wildest and most intractable of all the Pathans. About 100,000 Mahsuds live within two score miles of Kanigurum. In the bustling village has been brewed some of the wildest mischief ever let loose on the Frontier.

One of Kanigurum's most notorious inhabitants, still remembered by many Mahsuds, was a suave young Arab of the famous Gilani family, which together with al Hajj Amin Husseini, the Grand Mufti of Jerusalem, promoted Hitler's cause all over the Middle East in the 1930s.

This young man appeared in Waziristan in 1938. Dressed in the robes of a Muslim scholar and exploiting the Mahsuds' reverence for the holy places of Islam, he preached widely amongst the tribe and won the title of the *Shami Pir*, 'the Syrian Saint'. The area was still seething from the troubles of 1936 and 1937 and the *Shami Pir* had little trouble in raising a *lashkar* to avenge a host of real and fancied wrongs.

He quickly turned the *lashkar* to the purpose of restoring King Amanulla to the throne of Kabul. It did not bother the Mahsuds in the slightest that less than ten years earlier they had played a leading rôle in placing King Nadir Shah upon Amanulla's throne; happily whetting their knives, the tribesmen began to move across the Afghan Border.

By this time word of the *Shami Pir*'s activities had reached the British authorities. They quickly concluded that the replacement of the generally neutralist Afghan Government under Nadir Shah's son, Zahir, by the reportedly pro-German Amanulla (long resident in Italy) did not augur well for the security of India in a world rushing towards the Second World War.

By a masterpiece of diplomatic and para-military action, the *Shami Pir* was plucked from the midst of his Mahsuds, put into an aeroplane with £20,000 in gold to console him, and deposited back in Syria. Lacking leadership, the *lashkar* soon dispersed, and Zahir Shah and his government remained benignly neutral during the 1939–1945 hostilities.

The details of the operation by which the *Shami Pir* was removed remain secret even today, and the most garrulous reminiscences of old British Frontier hands stop abruptly when the conversation turns to the subject.

As for the Mahsuds themselves, their ferocity radiates from them in an almost physical way which sets them off even from their wild brethren. The young men at their most charming, with a flower tucked behind their ears and a wide grin on their lips, betray a restlessness and a pent-up violence. One feels that the volcano may erupt at any moment and one tends to sit far enough away to have a chance at least of not being consumed in the explosion.

The old men, like their peers in other tribes, present an appearance of profound dignity. Yet with them too there is a smouldering sub-surface, which betrays itself occasionally in small restless movements and mutterings, very unlike the serene calm which the Afridi elders affect so strikingly.

When talking about themselves, the Mahsuds use a phrase uniquely their own: *Mizh Mahsudi*, 'We Mahsuds', or sometimes *Mizh dhri Mahsudi*, 'We three Mahsuds', that is, the three great sub-sections of the Mahsud tribe, the Bahlolzai, Alizai, and Shaman Khel. While the phrase—and the arrogant grin which usually accompanies it—is apt in conveying the shared ferocity of the tribe, it is not particularly appropriate in so far as political organisation is concerned.

There are more *maliks* amongst the Mahsuds than amongst many of the other tribes and they have less authority. There are also more mullas, and the priestly craft is not left, as it is amongst the Yusufzai, for example, to non-members of the tribe. There is little horizontal organisation amongst the many clans and families, and certainly no *malik* or group of *maliks* who can speak for the whole tribe. Indeed at one time the British, in trying to devise a system for dealing with the tribe, were forced to fall back on the creation of an abstract concept: 'the Mahsud Jirga', which consisted of almost 20,000 members, that is, just about every adult male in the area.

One might think from all this that the Mahsuds lack a sense of humour. One story about them suggests that this is not the case.

Lord Linlithgow, Viceroy of India in the late Thirties, was a devoted agriculturalist and husbandman. He was struck, as many others have been, by the poor quality of the meat-producing animals in India and resolved to do something to improve the food supply, at least in the Muslim areas where beef was an acceptable item for consumption.

In hope of restoring some vigour to the sad strains of cattle, the viceroy imported champion bulls from England. With considerable fanfare, these animals were transported to various points in the country where their services were offered free to the local cows.

One of the prize bulls was brought to Waziristan. Like everything else of value in that turbulent country, it was quartered for the night within the confines of a heavily guarded cantonment. In the morning, to the consternation of all, the viceregal bull was gone.

Days later, after frantic cables to Delhi had been dispatched and all the resources of the political service thrown into the search, a note was delivered to the political agent. Written in passable English, the note formally conveyed the compliments of the Mahsuds to the viceroy, expressed their appreciation for his interest in the diet of the Pathans, and ended with the statement: 'Some of our people who have served your king have long told us of the wonderful music you play in your mess called "The roast beef of old England". Thanks to the favour of the Honourable

Viceroy we now know, for the first time, the true meaning of this song.'

The political agent for South Waziristan has his winter headquarters at Tank in Dera Ismail Khan District; his summer headquarters are at Wana, in the heart of South Waziristan. Wana is a neat little cantonment, but the place has had a bloody history ever since one of Sir Mortimer Durand's boundary commission camps was sacked and burned there in 1894.

Wana has always been a hard place to get to. For years it was not a 'family' station, that is, officers stationed there could not have their families with them. There is no public transport, and the traveller has to depend on official transport as well as hospitality. There are still stories about daring young British girls in the Thirties who disguised themselves as subalterns in order to ride up with a convoy and lay claim to having been one of the rare women to penetrate the farthest post on the Frontier. (Their husbands or fiancés usually had an unpleasant interview with the political agent afterwards.)

When I asked for permission to visit Wana in Peshawar, I was told that the state of the road was influenced by 'local conditions' and that its control was the responsibility of the political agent then resident at Tank. When I arrived in Tank one day late in November, the political agent told me that permission had to be granted by the Governor's office in Peshawar.

"So what do I do now?" I asked.

"Nothing," he said, picking up the phone. "I will get you permission. I will also go with you."

It was arranged that we would spend the night at Wana, which would make me, as far as the local records showed, the first American who had slept there. We set out early in the morning with the usual lorries of *khassadars* before and behind. The road, one of the most strategic links in the Frontier net, runs almost due west for more than sixty miles. Wana, at the far end, represents the deepest permanent penetration of the Frontier which the British made.

Our driver, a stout, jovial *khassadar* of early middle age, described the various points of interest as we went along. His accounts were simple and violent: "On that hill Wazir Khan killed two Mahsuds five years ago." "That *nulla* there is where my brother and I ambushed a British officer—one of those who wear skirts—when we were still less than twenty." "At the next turn the political agent sahib was fired at last year and I saved him by my skilful driving."

It was obvious that the *khassadar* was an old retainer of the political agent and he treated him with the peculiar mixture of respect, affection, and equality at which Pathans of all stations are so adept.

When we were passing the fort at Jandola the political agent turned the tables, asking, with a grin, "And what terrible thing happened there?"

The driver laughed uproariously. After a few pungent remarks in very colloquial Pushtu, he gave all his attention to the road.

"He spent some time behind bars up there," the political agent explained. "He was a very famous *badmash* [outlaw] until we became friends some years ago."

The Shahur Tangi is a defile so narrow that even at mid-day the road through it is in nearly complete shadow. Shattered rock faces rise up on both sides to saw-tooth cliffs. A few even narrower *nullas* (ravines) branch off at angles to the main defile. To Pathans, whose study of the art of ambush has been wide and deep, it is a perfect trap for the unwary.

A column moving through must narrow and stretch out. There is no place to dig in or form lines. There is no room for vehicles to turn around and no place for them to hide. Ten thousand boulders are ready-made for snipers and it is impossible to maintain scouts on the flanks. The rock faces can be occupied and evacuated by hundreds of men in a few minutes.

A bullet through the windshield of the first lorry stops the whole convoy. Then one has the choice of picking off the desperate soldiers who tumble out to kneel in the road or driving them with volleys into the side *nullas* where your fellows can do even more devastating work with their knives. There is additional excitement to be had by shooting at the petrol-tanks of the halted lorries. When one is hit the flames and heat form an impenetrable barrier between the rock faces and the defenders are cut off from one another.

The Shahur Tangi has figured prominently in almost every disturbance in Waziristan for a hundred years. Its classic moment, however, came early on an April morning in 1937 when a fifty-vehicle convoy was moving from Jandola to Wana. Escorted by four armoured-cars and about one hundred and fifty troops, the convoy was caught in the middle of the defile by a *lashkar* of some seventy Mahsuds. Later on in the day British reinforcements arrived from Sarwekai and Wana, and tribesmen from neighbouring villages joined the *lashkar* until some three hundred Pathans were involved. Before night fell the British had lost forty-seven killed and fifty wounded, almost all members of the original convoy escort. The tribesmen suffered sixteen killed and twenty-six wounded.

The political agent was still describing the fine points of this action some time after we had left the defile when his attention was caught by a procession of tribesmen marching along the road carrying a shrouded form on a *charpoy* (cot) in the manner of funerals all over the Frontier. The bearers were not armed—in itself a fact to inspire wonder in Waziristan.

We stopped and exchanged solemn salutes. The bearers put the cot down and the political agent leaned over and pulled the covering back from the face of the man who lay on it. He said something in rapid Pushtu and to my surprise and relief received an answer.

It appeared that the man on the cot was a Wazir down with a particularly virulent case of recurrent malaria. Even as the cot stood on the ground it shook with his violent trembling, and his words were literally tumbled from his twisted lips.

"They are taking him to a village up here a way," the political agent explained, "where there is a *hakim* who is said to be able to cure these cases. The *hakim* could not come to their village because there are some people there who have a feud with him and might kill him. They are, therefore, taking the sick man to the *hakim*'s village in a peaceful manner."

He turned back and argued with the bearers. They seemed to be on the verge of agreement when the figure on the cot protested. The political agent expostulated briefly, shook his shoulders, and returned to the car where he started digging in the boot.

"I tried to get them to let us take him to the hospital in Wana," he said, "but he won't go. He has some enemies near Wana who killed his father and he is afraid that they will find him when he is sick. So we will just have to give him some quinine here."

He broke open a large cardboard case and gave some packets of pills to the tribesmen, indicating that several of them were for the sick man. The tribesmen, obviously needing no explanation in their use, received the tablets eagerly. They picked up their burden and jogged on down the road with the patient feebly waving his thanks from the bouncing *charpoy*.

I remarked on the large supply of quinine the political agent carried. "I thought it best to give each of them a few tablets for themselves, so that they would not try to save some from what that poor fellow needs," he explained. "They practically all have malaria and quinine is the only medicine they really respect."

"Wait until we pass through these villages up here," he added, "and you'll see why I carry so much of the stuff. It's better than candy for winning friends and does some good to boot. Besides, the agency budget doesn't provide for candy."

A little farther along the car was surrounded by children piping, "Quinine, quinine!" We passed out the tablets with a liberal hand, the driver scattering them about at the same time as he loudly threatened to run over the 'little imps'. This was apparently a familiar performance and the children obviously looked upon both *khassadar* and political agent with trust and affection. What they thought of me I never knew, but I managed to get rid of a fair share of tablets also.

"They certainly seem fond of you," I remarked as we pulled clear of the mob. Then, remembering the driver's earlier remark, I asked, "What's this about someone trying to shoot you last year?"

"Shoot me?" The political agent looked surprised.

"Yes, your *khassadar* said he saved you."

"O," he grinned. "He was just boasting for your benefit. Sometimes a man who is dissatisfied over something, maybe at the size of his allowance, will fire at me to show his displeasure, but none of our people would ever really try to hit me.

"As a matter of fact, though, this business last year was a bit different. It was in Wazir territory that the shots were fired. I knew none of the Wazirs had anything to be displeased with me about at the time, so I soon figured out that the culprit was a Mahsud who had a feud with the Wazirs and had sneaked into their territory to fire at me in the hope that they would be blamed.

"By the way," he added comfortingly, "you know you are perfectly safe here. No one has any reason to be displeased with you, and the only reason someone might take a shot at you would be to get his enemy in trouble. Even then he wouldn't hit you because that would make not only the Government but the people in whose territory you were in very angry."

Such subtleties in matters of life and death are traditional in Waziristan. In the days after the First World War, when the British began to use aircraft to strafe or bomb inaccessible hostiles, an occasional biplane would fall victim to a sharpshooting tribesman. The Wazirs did not consider the use of aircraft entirely sporting and the treatment meted out to the captured airman was inevitably painful and frequently fatal.

This loss of machine—and skilled pilot—was very much a case of what Kipling used to call 'arithmetic on the Frontier': 'two thousand pounds of education drops to a ten-rupee *jezail* [musket]'. The RAF, resourceful then as now, soon devised a way to reduce its losses—at least its human ones. A generous bounty was offered for shot-down airmen, the exact amount varying according to the condition in which they were returned.

If this gave the tribesmen increased zest in potting at aircraft, it also greatly reduced pilot loss and restored relations between enemies to the honourable state in which they had been before the British took to the air. Indeed, it tended to make the aeroplane the safest mode of attack against the Pathans.

Wana itself lies in a small plain, the focal point of a number of long-standing feuds between the resident Wazirs and the encroaching, land-hungry Mahsuds. Some bits of ground have been fought over so often that very nearly as much blood has been spilled on them as rain has fallen from the usually cloudless skies.

The double-walled cantonment has an air of peace, however, and the scent of its tidy English gardens was fragrant even in the chill twilight of approaching winter. We had an early dinner in the South Waziristan Scouts Mess (this time I had brought my dinner-jacket) and afterwards listened to Radio Kabul, "The only really entertaining thing there is to do here in an evening," explained an officer resplendent in blue and gold dress-uniform.

The Afghan announcer did not fail us. After a more or less factual round-up of World and local news, he gave a long report of the doings of the 'Pushtoon freedom fighters', who, he said, were everywhere defying the rule of repressive Pakistani officials in their fight for an independent 'Pushtoonistan'. He ended with a stirring account of an attack on Wana the previous night which had left "that stronghold of the Pakistani imperialists" empty and burning.

"That's the third time this year we have been wiped out," said the Scouts officer. "Unless you listen to Kabul Radio, you can have no idea how dangerous it is here."

Later we strolled through the few short streets of the cantonment and stopped for a final smoke on a wall looking out west towards the broken vastness of Afghanistan. Far away, over the Dasht-i-Margo, the 'Desert of Death', there was a final deep red, almost maroon, glow in the dark blue sky from the sun which must have already been beginning to sink in the Iranian sky.

The occasional sounds of men under arms came through the soft darkness: the clash of a rifle barrel on a bandolier, the scrape of a dagger against a wall, the clatter of a rifle being disassembled in the Scouts barracks below. A young *khassadar* from the political agent's escort leaned in a corner of the wall, his attention fixed casually on us while his hawk's eyes stared unblinkingly out over the dim landscape.

One of the officers from the mess who had accompanied us stood beside me. Familiar as it must have been, the scene obviously still held a fascination for him also.

"It's a beautiful place," I said, "a pity you do not bring your families."

He looked around slowly, savouring the atmosphere, before replying.

"A great pity, indeed," he agreed, without a trace of a smile but with a mischievous twinkle in his eyes.

The Malakand Pass, with the Swat Canal in the foreground

(*Left*) The Buddhist ruins at Takht-i-Bhai

(*Below*) The author's wife on a home-made raft on the River Indus at Rana Dheri

XIV

'Zan'

WHEN I HAD FINISHED the thirteen chapters which have gone before, I felt that I had pretty well covered all the more important and interesting specific aspects of the Pathans as such. Now, I thought, I could talk about broader matters: their relations with Pakistan, Afghanistan, and the World at large.

Before carrying on, however, I asked my wife to look over what I had written. Having done so, Edith said that she was reminded of the story about the prominent public figure who had written his autobiography: he had told of his birth, his boyhood struggles, his rise to fame, the influential people he had known, the great things he himself had done and said and written. Then he asked his wife to read his manuscript. She did, and she said that she was curious about only one thing: "Was your hero ever married?"

This is not an autobiography and Edith does appear in the preceding pages. However, it must be admitted that hardly anything is said about *zan*, the women of the Frontier, and the reader might well ask at this point: "Do your heroes ever marry?"

They do, of course, and they have not only wives but mothers, sisters, daughters, aunts, nieces and female cousins. They speak very little about women, however, whether their own or anyone else's, and the strictly masculine atmosphere of the preceding pages is in that sense representative of real life.

There are a few things which can be said about Pathan women, although I must confess that they come more from Edith's experience and intuition than from my own.

In the first place, one thing which the Pathans do proclaim freely is that their women are as brave, resourceful and, above all, as honourable, as themselves. Tribal women are trained to use a rifle, and all the traditional Islamic restrictions on their actions and contacts—which most Pathans ordinarily observe with extreme strictness—are relaxed in times of war or emergency.

More sophisticated women of the towns and the plains are frequently well educated, and in matters of business or politics affecting their families are wont to offer—and often enforce—their shrewd advice. Tribal and town alike, the women generally are even more devoted to the requirements of honour than their men, and more than one Pathan who left to himself would have found a practical equivocation to settle his problems has found himself reluctantly playing the gallant to still the urgings of his womenfolk.

For the most part the women of the Frontier are part of the background only. It is true that the Western visitor is at first acutely aware of the shrouded figures in their tent-like *burqas* who may be seen flitting about the bazaars. When he sits down for a meal, he cannot help but be struck with the profusion and tastiness of the food and impressed with the abilities of the mistress of the house who is responsible for it—invisible though she is. Finally, of course, there are the large troops of children who—especially the charming little girls—are convincing evidence of the existence of another sex in Pathan life.

Soon the male visitor tends to become oblivious to the existence of women in the daily life of the community, however important his own women may be in his own private life. In this he is at one with his Pathan hosts.

For most Pathan women a bustling though isolated life goes on behind the purda (veil). For some, of course, the purda does not exist: the wives and daughters of the *powendas* on their perpetual migration, the women of the poorer tribesmen who must work the fields and tend the animals, a handful of the more daring wives of liberal-minded officials.

A few have the best of both worlds, abandoning the veil while away from the Frontier and flitting back and forth around it while at home. One of these 'was sitting with us in mixed company, chatting gaily and urbanely over tea, when a caller knocked at the door. She excused herself rapidly and invited Edith upstairs before the new arrival entered.

To Edith's "O, I didn't know you observed purda," she gave the scornful answer:

"Only for *that* man—my husband's boss."

Another close friend, the wife of a political official, talented, widely travelled, and professionally trained, produced a *burqa* from her handbag and reluctantly donned it when the car in which she and Edith were riding crossed into tribal territory. Nodding her shrouded head at some tribesmen by the side of the road, she explained, "My husband is responsible for them, you know, and if he is to do anything, he must have their respect."

One of Edith's gayest memories is of a ladies' party on the Indus River near Dera Ismail Khan. She and her hostess had driven some thirty miles to participate in the event. A large launch nosed about amongst the many channels of the great river while the ladies drank tea, gossiped, and compared jewellery and clothes. Being unusually cosmopolitan they did not, I am told, compare their husbands' salaries, official positions, and prospects for promotion. When they got back to shore they played badminton before setting out again to drive back to their homes scattered over a hundred miles of territory.

There is, of course, a more austere side to the life of Pathan women. A glimpse of it may be had—by female visitors only—at the women's hospital at Tank on the edge of South Waziristan. This remarkable institution consists of a collection of low adobe buildings scattered about a slightly untidy garden. When we first visited Tank the hospital was run by a delightful quartet of English ladies with missionary connections. They received guests in a crowded, comfortable little parlour, with an air of rural England about it, which appeared to have changed little in the quarter of a century during which they had ministered to the woefully neglected health of the women of Dera Ismail Khan District and South Waziristan.

One of the wards is a memorial to Duncan, the young British political agent who was killed by a Mahsud in 1948 not a hundred yards away. There is no air of gloom about it, however. Upon entering, Edith was embraced by the ward assistant, a jovial, robust tribal girl of about fifteen, who commented pungently on the doctor's description of the patients' ailments as she walked from bed to bed.

Except for a few in the surgical ward, the beds are typical Pathan *charpoys*. The patients do not wear conventional hospital gowns. To the Pathans an all-white costume means only one thing: a shroud. However, they cheerfully wear a kind of uniform offered by the hospital, a blue *kameez* (dress) over the usual baggy pyjama-trousers. As a special feminine touch, each ward has a different colour *dupatta* (scarf). In Duncan's Ward, the *dupattas* were a gay orange.

The wealthier women bring their own servants; almost all the patients have at least one family member in attendance. Outside the wards are rows of charcoal hearths where each patient's servants or relatives prepare her food. Some bring their own provisions. For those who cannot afford to do so, grain and vegetables from the garden are supplied by the hospital.

There are few gunshot wounds in the women's hospital—for to shoot a woman is considered an act of great cowardice. Most of the cases are 'fever', which in the vocabulary of the patients covers everything from the endemic malaria to rare organic diseases and obstetrical problems. Normal deliveries are few in the hospital—for if there are no complications, why would a woman go to the hospital merely to have a baby?

The poor diet of many of the tribal women accounts for the prevalence of rickets and other bone diseases. Caesarean deliveries were routine, even in the mobile dispensary which the medical ladies took to the Wana area in the summer. Underlying all the happy bustle and healing art of the hospital is the sad fact that life in the hills is especially hard on women and that many of the patients would not be there at all but for want of proper diet and treatment in their daily lives.

I remarked earlier that the most common causes of breach of the peace on the Frontier are *zar* (gold), *zan* (woman) and *zamin* (land). *Zan* may play a remarkably inconspicuous rôle in public life and is seldom mentioned in the public press. However, women are very much a part of the legal records.

The wise and gentle advocate-general in Peshawar has drawn from his long experience as a public prosecutor a collection of cases categorised according to the types and motives of murder. In a great many of them women are the focal point, though usually in a passive rôle.

There was, for example, the case of Sharif Khatoon and Nur Jehan, mistress and wife, respectively, of one Fateh Khan, who met their deaths a few years ago at their betrayer's hands. Their story, and that of their menfolk, is as convoluted as an Icelandic saga. To try to reduce it to its essentials, it is best to focus on its long-suffering hero, Nur Khan, boyhood friend of the murderer, who was a soldier in the army.

After the Second World War in which he had seen service in North Africa against Rommel, Nur Khan returned for a visit to his native village. While there, he married the sister of his long-time friend, Fateh Khan, and took her back to his garrison town. At first the young couple were happy, but soon they fell to quarrelling and eventually were divorced.

This cast a pall over relations between Nur Khan and Fateh Khan, but after a few years the unpleasantness seemed to have been forgotten. When Nur Khan came back again on leave to his village he was constantly with Fateh Khan. When he decided to marry again and selected the beautiful Sharif Khatoon, Fateh Khan arranged the wedding. At the time there were no quarters for married soldiers at Nur Khan's post and he left Sharif Khatoon in his mother's house, asking his old friend, Fateh Khan, to help look after her.

The seeds of tragedy were soon sown. Fateh Khan fell in love with Sharif Khatoon. Fateh Khan's own wife, Nur Jehan, wrote to Nur Khan at his army post warning him that he must return if his honour was not to be outraged. Stung with jealousy and rage, Nur Khan decided that this was his friend's revenge for his having divorced Fateh Khan's sister a decade earlier. He rushed home, denounced Fateh Khan before the villagers, and sent for his errant wife's father and brother to come to take her home with them. In doing this, he was acting with unusual self-control and moderation, since, under the Pathan code, he had already the undeniable right to kill both his wife and his friend.

A day or so later the sobbing Sharif Khatoon set out with her father and her brother, who remained on the best of terms with Nur Khan, being grateful to him for having spared the guilty girl. Nur Khan himself accompanied them for a way to get a bus back to his camp. While the three men tarried at the bus-stop, Sharif Khatoon went on ahead alone.

She had not gone far when Fateh Khan, who had been follow-ing the party, overtook her. He demanded that she return to her husband's house so that their liaison could continue. When she refused, saying that he had already dishonoured her enough, he killed her with an axe he was carrying. Her father and brother, coming along a few minutes later, discovered the body in the road.

Meanwhile, Fateh Khan returned to his village. Storming into his house he denounced his own wife, Nur Jehan, for making known his guilt, and killed her with the axe still stained with the blood of Sharif Khatoon. He was overpowered by the villagers and eventually brought to trial for the double murder. Nur Khan was a deadly and implacable witness, and spent his own time and money liberally to help produce evidence against the murderer. After Fateh Khan was found guilty and hanged, however, Nur Khan, in a typical Pathan gesture, adopted the little orphan daughter of Fateh Khan and Nur Jehan, as he said, in memory of the happy days he had had long ago with his friend and his friend's sister who had been his first wife.

Another tale from the advocate-general's chronicles has less of the flavour of a Gothic novel. Indeed, its simple and straightforward plot and final triumph of right over might makes it more like a Victorian melodrama, or perhaps, more aptly, a medieval morality play. Remarkably, its hero and chief actor is a woman.

Habib Nur was a poor Pathan girl married to her equally impoverished cousin. She was beautiful and he was strong, and by all accounts the young couple were devoted to each other; their lives ran happily enough until they were struck almost simultaneously with a double misfortune: the course of the river shifted and inundated their small field and the husband fell ill and was unable to work even as a share-cropper.

On the verge of penury, Habib Nur put aside her pride (it was considered dishonourable for a married Pathan women under any circumstances to work for anyone other than her husband) and got a job at the local primary school as a chaperone.

It was part of her job to pick up the schoolgirls in the morning and to accompany them back to their homes in the evening. In the course of her daily travels through the village, Habib Nur caught the eye of Zain Khan, a rich young man-about-town. He pursued her constantly, eventually telling her that he would pay her husband 5,000 rupees compensation if she would elope with him.

Habib Nur complained to the elders of the village, who tried to get Zain Khan to stop his dishonourable activities—but he

would not. Finally Habib Nur, to avoid trouble, gave up her job
and moved with her sick husband to another village a few miles
away. Their poverty there was even more acute, but they
managed to stay together, and were sleeping one night in their
poor hut when the door was broken in by Zain Khan and his
servants.

The servants hurled themselves upon the husband and Zain
Khan seized Habib Nur. Twisting away, she snatched an axe from
the corner and with a single stroke cleft her assailant's skull so
deeply that the axe blade could not be extracted. The servants fled
and soon the police arrived. They had no choice but to charge her
with 'culpable homicide not amounting to murder', and a day
was set for trial at Abbottabad, the district headquarters.

News of the case spread far and wide, and when the day arrived
the court had to move from its usual place to the Town Hall in
order to accommodate even a portion of the hundreds who had
come to the town. When Habib Nur was led into the court, the
spectators rose and cheered. The numerous witnesses called by
the prosecutor all testified eloquently to Habib Nur's virtue and
courage. She herself made no defence. The prosecutor briefly
described the right of self-defence. The judge did not even consider it necessary to call on defence counsel to reply. The assessors
(jurors) declared with a single voice their verdict of 'not guilty!'

The ensuing hubbub was quieted by the public prosecutor, who
proposed that a subscription be raised for Habib Nur in appreciation of her bravery. Judge and jury joined in the contributions
and more than 2,000 rupees were collected on the spot. Habib
Nur and her husband were garlanded and taken back in a procession to their village where they used the money they had been
given to buy land. And they lived happily ever after?

Yes, they did. All this happened in 1934. A quarter of a century
later the young prosecutor who had proposed the subscription,
now the dignified advocate-general, went back to Habib Nur's
little village and found her and her three stalwart sons prospering;
they were devoted to the memory of the husband and father who
had died not long before.

The Western visitor—the male one at least—may readily become oblivious to women when he is actually on the Frontier.
However, in looking back as I am doing now, he finds a curious
sense of frustration over his meagre knowledge of this facet of

Pathan life. Thus, I am tempted to apologise for depending so heavily in my descriptions on second-hand accounts of this obviously vital part of Frontier society.

Yet, stories and legends—and often the one merges quickly and imperceptibly into the other—are so essential a part of the Pathan way of life that perhaps no apology is necessary after all. And certainly, in story and legend at least, Pathan women play as important a rôle as they deserve. Before we leave the subject consider, for example, the story of Shabeena and Motamar, a life and death drama which was played out in flesh and blood less than half a dozen years ago but which is already part of a legend that will be as fresh a hundred years hence as it is now.

Shabeena (Flower of the Night) was the younger daughter of an influential *malik* in Dir. She was beautiful, fragile and innocent, and her life was destined from an early age to be touched with heroic tragedy. Her elder sister was one of the wives of the old and despotic nawab, and when Shabeena went to stay with her sister for some weeks in the palace *zenana*, the covetous eye of the nawab was entranced with her youth and charm.

Her sister sensed this and quickly sent to their father asking that Shabeena be brought home before the greatest disgrace fell upon the family, for according to local custom, for a man to marry his wife's sister is the equivalent of incest—abominable dishonour for all concerned.

This did not bother the nawab, but Shabeena's father speedily hurried her home to the safety of his own women's quarters. To hinder the evil intentions of the nawab, the father forthwith set out to find a suitable young husband for Shabeena. Everyone he approached, however, was immediately contacted also by the retainers of the nawab, who made clear the dire fate which awaited anyone so rash as to be a party to frustrating their master's desire to have Shabeena for his own. No matter how rich a dowry her father offered, no matter how great her own beauty, no husband could be found amongst the leading families of the area who was willing to risk the nawab's displeasure.

Finally the father, desperate to preserve the family honour, thought of Motamar, a well-known outlaw of the hills, simple and unsophisticated but brave and dashing. Motamar was approached and the offer of betrothal made. Motamar had heard of the beauty and charm of Shabeena and he feared neither devil,

man, nor nawab. And so the pampered chieftain's daughter and
the rough outlaw were married. Amidst the rejoicing of the
wedding the stern chieftain, ever-mindful of his family's honour,
extracted from Motamar the sombre promise that, if ever it were
necessary, he would kill his young wife rather than let her fall
into the hands of the nawab.

The honeymoon at Motamar's crude fortress in the hills was
happy but brief. After a few weeks the nawab sent thirty of his
men in an armed attack to recover Shabeena. Motamar and his
followers beat off the assault, but they knew they could not with-
stand the army that would follow. So Motamar, his father, and
two brothers, Shabeena, and a maidservant trekked over one of
the high, unmarked passes of the mountains into Chitral State.
There they requested sanctuary of the political agent who represented the Pakistani Government, and were put up in the guest-
house of the ruler of Chitral, conveniently an ancient enemy of
the nawab of Dir.

Frustrated in the use of force, the nawab now turned to guile.
Producing a few perjured witnesses from amongst his minions,
he claimed that Shabeena had been married to one of his lieu-
tenants, and that she had illegally been abducted by Motamar.
The 'husband' was temporarily ill said the nawab, but Shabeena
obviously must be returned to his state at once where she would
be under his personal care.

By this time the story of Motamar and Shabeena was widely
known and the political agent, himself a Pathan, was in a difficult
spot. It was his job to keep the peace, and to defy the powerful
nawab would have had exactly the opposite effect. At the same
time he had given sanctuary to the fleeing couple and his honour
and future effectiveness amongst the tribesmen were deeply involved in their safety. He sent back word to the nawab that he
would convoke a meeting of mullas (priests) to decide the difficult
case. He had to agree, however, to the nawab's demand that
pending the verdict of the mullas Motamar and Shabeena were
to be separated.

The ruler of Chitral readily agreed to take Shabeena into his
own palace to protect her until the verdict was given. Motamar,
however, willing to trust no one but himself, made it clear that
he would not suffer any kind of separation from his beloved, and
it was necessary for the political agent to take him by stealth and

lodge him in the local jail. The problem still remained of getting Shabeena away from Motamar's father and brothers who were now guarding her in his stead.

An effort was made to drug their evening meal, but a sympathetic cook warned them. Consequently, when the political agent's men came to take the girl to the protection of the ruler of Chitral, they were met with unexpected resistance. When the ensuing fight began to go against Motamar's kinsmen, one of his brothers, fulfilling his promise, killed Shabeena. A few moments later, he himself fell mortally wounded.

Within an hour news of the tragedy had reached Motamar in his cell, whereupon he broke jail and headed for Dir to take his revenge on the nawab. Fortunately for the peace of the border he was intercepted before he got there and returned to Chitral, where he was put under guard and bound over to keep the peace.

All of Chitral walked in Shabeena's funeral procession, and a few days later holy and mysterious lights were seen at her tomb as darkness fell. Thus, the fame of her beauty and virtue and admiration of her destiny to suffer death before dishonour spread all over the Frontier; it was not long before the little flags which mark the tomb of a saint flew over her grave, and the ladies of the neighbourhood came there on Friday afternoons to talk and pray that they too might live and die in noble virtue.

And Shabeena's plentitudinous honour was shared by Motamar and his kinsmen, who were given a generous grant of land and who live on in Chitral enjoying the respect and dignity accorded to brave and honourable Pathans.

XV

Progress with Pakistan

WHEN I RETURNED to Pakistan as a private citizen on a Ford Foundation fellowship, I was required to register with the police. This I did in Karachi shortly after my arrival. I was given a large form which recognised my right to be in the country and I was told that whenever I changed my residence for more than twenty-four hours, I must present the form to the local police. The same injunction was printed (with a good many others) on the back of the form.

In due course I moved from Karachi to Lahore, then on to Peshawar and the Khyber, to Kohat and Kurrum, Bannu and Waziristan, Mardan and Malakand, with a day or two at a dozen more obscure places in between. Later I moved on to Hazara, over the mountains to Gilgit, back to Rawalpindi, and then to Peshawar again with a view to crossing the Durand Line into Afghanistan. Most irresponsibly, I failed to visit a single police-station anywhere on this two-month-long *hegira*. It was partly because I was forgetful, partly that I was still in the habit of my diplomatic days when such regulations did not apply, and partly that as I went about seeing old friends, talking to high officials, and freely receiving permission to do all that I wanted, I simply could not believe that the grubby business of reporting to the police every other day was meant to apply to me. But mostly, I fear, I was just careless.

At length, as I was about to leave for Afghanistan, I realised that I would need police approval of my exit before crossing the international border. With considerable trepidation, I dug out the form I had received in Karachi and took myself off to police headquarters in Peshawar Cantonment.

I had not made an appointment, but it was a quiet weekday afternoon and after a few minutes prowling about I found a door with a small sign reading, 'Alien registration: exit permits.' Inside, an inspector of police sat at a table, all alone in the middle of a pleasantly uncluttered room. The table was bare except for an old-fashioned pen and ink-pot, a pad of official forms, and a fly-switch.

The inspector offered me a chair with great courtesy. I passed over my passport and, with an inner tremor, my police form. After the most casual of glances, he filled in the space at the bottom of the form authorising my exit and re-entry into Pakistan.

"You have had a pleasant time in Pakistan?" he inquired, beaming.

"Yes, indeed," I replied.

"In Peshawar?"

"O, yes."

"It was a pity, though, that you had to wait in Rawalpindi so long for the plane to Gilgit."

"O, well . . ."

"But you found some interesting pieces of sculpture in Swat."

"Uh mm."

"Those Mahsuds in the Tank bazaar, I hope they did not over-charge you for that dagger."

"Uh mm."

"And your ankle has recovered from the sprain you got on the road near Thal?"

"Quite recovered, thank you."

The gentle catechism continued, paralleling almost perfectly my itinerary and activities of the preceding eight weeks. At the end, the inspector passed the registration form back to me and said with a grin, "You will want this when you return. There are instructions and things on the back. You really should read them. I hope you have a pleasant time in Afghanistan."

"Thank you," I said—and fled.

There were two morals to be drawn from the incident, I decided. The first and most obvious was that Pakistani officials, like most of their countrymen, are a friendly and courteous lot, not lacking a sense of humour. They administer the sometimes archaic and arbitrary regulations and customs of their country with an urbane tolerance befitting free and self-confident men. The second lesson lay in what struck me as a remarkable parallel between the way the government of Pakistan governs the Frontier visitor—myself in this case—and the way it governs the Frontier. For this purpose there exists, in addition to the normal laws of

Pakistan, a whole host of special provisions for the maintenance of peace in the turbulent borderland. The Frontier Crimes Regulations of 1901 (which in a modified form are still in effect) provide that the Government may seize and detain the persons and property of all or any members of a tribe which acts in a 'hostile or unfriendly manner' towards the Government; it may also confiscate such property and debar all members of the tribe from intercourse or communication with the settled districts. The ordinary protection for individual rights afforded by judicial writs does not apply.

In addition, of course, there are long standing provisions under which entry into and departure from tribal territory is controlled by the Government, subsidies to tribes and individuals can be withheld or given by the political agents, and political demonstrations of virtually any kind can be banned. Behind all these regulations stands the very considerable and almost unavoidably visible power of the Army, the scout units of the Frontier Corps, and the para-military Frontier Constabulary.

Yet this formidable array of power and authority is used only rarely, and then with the greatest of moderation. The result is that in the midst of a welter of restrictive laws and obvious reminders of force, a remarkable air of freedom and a high degree of mutual respect exists between the Pathans and their government. Everyone knows everything about everyone else. There is sometimes anger and scorn, and occasionally plotting and counter-plotting of a most devious nature, but seldom, if ever, fear or repression.

The tone was set almost immediately after the Partition in 1947 when Pakistan withdrew all troops from the cantonments and forts in tribal territory, thereby making it clear to the tribesmen that their new country assumed there would be no need to coerce them on a grand scale or use force against them as a people. It was easier for the Pakistanis to do this, of course, than it would ever have been for the British.

In the first place, the long standing incitation to *jihad* (holy war) which the presence of the Christian British in the lowlands had provided was no longer there. In the second, the Pakistanis were—and for a while at least could afford to be—far less concerned about defending the gates of the subcontinent against the traditional Russian menace. Thus, they had no reason to want to preserve a wild and restless marchland. Finally, of course, the

troops were needed on the eastern border with India because of
the tension which had grown up out of the communal killings of
the Partition and the Kashmir dispute.

Unlike the Punjab and Bengal, the Frontier was spared most
of the horrors of the Partition. There were only a few small riots
and none of the disruption of communications and food supply
suffered in other parts of India and Pakistan. This is not to say,
however, that the great event passed unnoticed amongst the
Pathans. Most of the Hindus, who took care of much of the small
business and banking, left. In their place came large numbers of
Muslim refugees from India seeking a new life. Many brought
with them little more than the clothes on their backs.

A concerted effort was made to absorb the newcomers, and
Peshawar was never plagued with the sprawling refugee camps
which for years constituted an ugly blot on most of the other
cities of Pakistan. There was one incident, however, over which
Peshawaris still chuckle when they talk of the days after the
Partition.

A committee of Pathan women had been appointed under the
direction of the wives of British officials, a number of whom
stayed on to serve the government of Pakistan. Amongst their
good works, the ladies went to the railway and bus-stations to
welcome the refugees and to try to organise their rehabilitation.
A group of several dozen refugee women from Amritsar in the
East Punjab arrived on one train. Wretched, miserable, and
obviously without resources, they huddled in the *burqas* awaiting
direction or a kind word.

One of the senior British ladies who spoke a fair standard of
Urdu tried to reassure them. They were all welcome to Peshawar
and to Pakistan, she told them; they need have no fear for their
futures. Whatever they had done in their former homes, however
they had earned their living, whatever skills they had, they could
rest assured that there was a place for them in Peshawar and that
all facilities would be given them to continue their lives as they
had been before.

Just at this point, one of the Pathan members of the women's
committee came up and quickly drew the lady aside. Her sharp
eye, accustomed to subtle differences which even the *burqas* do not
conceal, had detected something that the enthusiastic welcomer
had missed. The newcomers, the Pathan explained euphemisti-

cally, were 'dancing-girls'. "Perhaps we should not commit ourselves to promoting their careers just yet," she added.

The great event of the early days of independence on the
Frontier was the Kashmir *jihad*. The maharaja of the princely
Himalayan state was a Hindu; most of his subjects were Muslims.
According to the normal standards by which the princely states
were acceding to Pakistan or India, Kashmir should have gone to
Pakistan. The maharaja, however, by shrewd manœuvring had
managed to work out a 'standstill agreement', under which he
delayed accession for a couple of months after independence was
declared.

At this point a revolt broke out amongst the Muslims of Poonch
in western Kashmir. The efficient *Dogra* troops (high caste Hindu
warriors) of the maharaja began a brutal suppression. Hundreds
of miles away, up and down the Frontier and into Afghanistan,
the Pathan tribesmen, who until this time had played no rôle in
the great events which were occurring around them, rose with
remarkable spontaneity and headed for Kashmir.

There was no discipline and little organisation to the movement. Some local officials, acting on their own, supplied food and
trucks; a few Muslim officers of the former Indian Army attached
themselves to the swarming tribesmen and tried to provide
leadership and direction. For the most part, though, it was the
tribesmen's show. For a week they carried all before them.
Scattering the maharaja's *Dogras*, they smashed through Muzza-
farabad, over the pass at Baramula, and down into the fairy-tale
Vale of Kashmir. Half a dozen miles from Srinagar, which with
its airfield was the key to the valley, they stopped for a few days
to digest their loot—and lost Kashmir for Pakistan.

Panic-stricken, the maharaja acceded to India and, while the
Pathans prowled aimlessly about the outskirts of Srinagar, a
company of Sikhs were flown in from India and the airfield
secured. Within a month the newly arrived trained and disciplined
reinforcements were able to drive the tribesmen back up and out
of the valley. The fighting went on in a desultory fashion for
another year, until a cease-fire line which left two-thirds of the
state in India's hands was agreed upon under the auspices of the
United Nations. There the Kashmir problem has rested ever since.

There were ugly incidents in the Kashmir war, for example,
the sack of Baramula by the Mahsuds which resulted in the deaths

of an English colonel, his wife, and a nun, as well as the looted vestment mentioned earlier which constituted my introduction to the Pathans. For the most part, however, it was clean, honest fighting for a cause, in which the principal loot was the arms of dead enemies.

Wherever the visitor goes on the Frontier the tribesmen, whether individually or in *jirgas*, talk of Kashmir. To the Westerner, whose impression of Kashmir is often only a vague memory of an issue that arises periodically to trouble the UN, the intensity of their feeling is a revelation. The tribesmen are proud of what they did, but in later years a note of increasing irritation has clouded their accounts. They are angry with the United Nations, with the United Kingdom, with the United States, because nothing has been done to reclaim Kashmir from India, of which the state is now constitutionally an integral part. They are often angry even with Pakistan because the Government has prevented them from reopening the battle themselves.

For a while I was at a loss to understand the intensity of this bitterness. The Pathans obviously do not have any special affection for the Kashmiris and they have little in common except that they are all Muslims. They speak of them (with the exception of the brave Poonchis, whom they admire) in the same patronising manner which they use towards the Bengalis and Sindhis and other lesser peoples of the lowlands. Finally one day when an old *malik* used the word *badal* (revenge) over and over again, I discerned the answer. He and many of his fellows had lost relatives in Kashmir and, since complete victory had been denied, honour still required that the losses be avenged. "Until it is," the patriarch said simply, "neither I, nor my sons, nor their sons, will ever sleep happily a single night."

By and large, the Pathans' relations with their new government of Pakistan has been a harmonious one. It has its base in the economic and social welfare programme which Pakistan has used to promote a gradual integration of the Frontier into the national life. Hospitals and schools have multiplied many times over in the settled districts in the past dozen years. With them have come better agricultural methods and new industries. Pathans of all levels of social and economic development have passed beyond the narrow Frontier stage to take their places—usually high, or they would not otherwise have left their beloved home—in other

Powendas on the march in the Tochi,
North Waziristan. (*Right*) *Powenda* boy

The game of *buskashi* in Kabul

Powenda encampment in the Kurrum

parts of Pakistan. In turn, from the Punjab, from Sind, and even from what appears to a Pathan to be the other side of the earth, from Bengal, other Pakistanis have come to the Frontier. Through their abilities and devotion to the welfare of the people, these fellow citizens have introduced a new note of tolerance into the Frontier outlook—without diminishing in the slightest, of course, the Pathans' own pride, still the fiercest in the World.

In so far as the settled districts are concerned, the results of Pakistan's policy of integration have been most successful. Giant strides were made in the first half a dozen years after the Partition under Chief Minister Khan Abdul Qaiyum Khan, a great bulk of a man who throbbed with all the vigour of the many dynamos he scattered about the Province. In 1955 Curzon's proud creation, the North-West Frontier province, was amalgamated with the Punjab, Sind, and Baluchistan into the single unit province of West Pakistan. While many Pathans were not altogether happy with the loss of their separate political identity, there was far less bitterness and obstructionism than one might have anticipated, and the six settled districts are still amongst the most productive and vigorous in all West Pakistan.

The status of the tribal area has changed relatively little, but Pakistan has also made considerable progress in promoting integration amongst the hill tribesmen. A few of the more accessible and better developed areas were incorporated into the Province even before 1955. As additional areas of cultivable land have come into being below the new dams on the plains, hillsmen have trickled down to lay aside their rifles for the plough. Others have yielded to the temptations of trade, and Mahsuds and Afridis may be found doing business in the bazaars of Peshawar, Kohat, and Tank. Practically every tribe now has at least one or two of its brightest boys in the colleges or the university.

Hospitals and schools—but not taxation—have been extended here and there into the hills under a more vigorous but yet more benign policy of 'peaceful penetration' than the British were ever able to achieve. One political agent, for example, has for years maintained—illegally—a scholarship fund which he finances by an unofficial levy on the salt-trade in his agency. Whenever the fund rises to the needed amount, another boy from the tribe goes off to school in the plains.

At the same time it must be remembered that there are places in the hills, some of them, the Tirah, for example, hardly a dozen miles from the centres of population and administration, into which government officials dare not go and over which sovereignty is exercised in name only. Until recently Bajaur, a wild stretch of country north of the Khyber between the Malakand Pass and the Durand Line, was one of these. Then in the autumn of 1960 a complicated many-sided quarrel flared up there involving both Pakistan and Afghanistan, as well as the local tribesmen. The upshot was that the Pakistan Army in a return to the 'forward policy' approach of earlier British days moved in and occupied parts of Bajaur and the princely state of Dir. Educational and medical services came in on the heels of the troops, but even so the Pakistan Air Force found it necessary to make several air attacks on dissident tribesmen during the first half of 1961.

These air attacks, incidentally, have been a part of the Frontier strategy almost since aircraft have been available. In less than an hour a plane can get untouched to a spot which would take ground troops a week and half a dozen skirmishes to reach. The raids, even if they are now made in modern jet-fighters, still follow a traditionally benevolent pattern.

The target is usually the house or hiding-place of the leader of the dissidents, for amongst the Pathans a leader's prestige is closely associated with his ability to defend his home. Leaflets are dropped in advance giving warning of the exact time and place of the bombing. Punctual to the second, the aircraft arrives and bombs or rockets the empty structure. The thick mud walls are extremely durable and several passes are usually necessary. This makes for an even better show for the attentive audience perched safely on the sides of the nearby hills. It is all a very gentlemanly affair and I recall vividly an occasion when a Pakistani pilot was explaining the procedure to an eager young Western military flyer on his way home from the war in Korea. The visitor suggested that perhaps they should consider using napalm sometimes. "My dear chap, really . . ." said the local airman with a shudder of horror. "You just don't understand!"

The process of change which has been going on at the Frontier for almost fifteen years is fascinating to a student of political and social organisation. It is easy to put one's finger on significant problems and milestones of progress. Yet, I at least find it difficult to draw any very definite conclusions about the broader meaning of it all.

There is the romantic Kiplingesque school of thought which scoffs at the idea that permanent change is taking place. Its advocates loathe the idea of the dashing tribesmen ever becoming well-disciplined, socially-conscious citizens. Sixty years ago, they point out, British troops penetrated into the Tirah and few other outsiders have returned since. Thirty years ago, Razmak was a thriving administrative centre. Today it is abandoned and Waziristan is as free and untamed as ever it was. The favourite lullabies of Pathan mothers are often still rhythmic listings of the names of the men whom their babies' fathers and grandfathers have killed.

Other observers, amongst them the distinguished Professor Arnold Toynbee (who surely has had more experience than most at trying to catch and pin down the major trends of history), see Pakistan's handling of the hill Pathans as one of the most successful integrations of peoples ever attempted. Bajaur, into which even imperial Britain with her solid base in India never penetrated, is now peacefully under administration they argue. The Afridis, those archetypes of the Pathans, no longer count their wealth and power in rifles but in the buses they supply for the lucrative carrying-trade of the plains.

There is something to this point of view, certainly. I heard it myself half a dozen years ago from a venerable *malik* sitting in a *hujra* near Fort Jamrud at the entrance to the Khyber—quite possibly the same one who more recently edified Professor Toynbee. There was a twinkle in the *malik*'s eye as he said it, and he was obviously pleased with himself. It may have been that his delight flowed solely from the financial well-being of his transport company, but I cou'd not help feeling that he was even more taken with the felicity and appropriateness of the little gem of social history that he was passing on to an appreciative listener. I rather doubt that the old chief had ever seriously considered whether he believed his aphorism, and I am very sceptical indeed that, if called upon to choose, he would yet willingly yield his rifles rather than his buses.

Where all of this leaves the Frontier as far as the great movements of history are concerned, I do not know. One thing is clear: Pakistan's policy towards the Frontier has been a humane and constructive one. The Pathans have never tasted the bitterness of denial of their existence by their government which the Kurds have experienced. Their language and customs have not been suppressed. They are free to rise as high and go as far in their country as they choose. Most of them know it, and consequently they have permitted and even welcomed change. The years ahead undoubtedly hold still more change. Yet I have an idea that in some ways, at least, this may be a case of 'the more things change, the more they remain the same'. And when one considers that personal honour, bravery, and hospitality are still Pathan hallmarks in a world which for the most part has come to prefer sanitation, sophistication, and organised recreation, who would have it otherwise?

XVI

The Afghan Charm

THERE ARE MANY pleasant places in Pakistan, and almost all
of the people I have met there—not just the Pathans—have
been attractive and interesting. I had got to know Pakistan's
people and places fairly well before it occurred to me that I should
also try to learn something of Afghanistan and the Afghans.

The atmosphere in Karachi was not very conducive to this
endeavour. Indeed, I was reminded of my days in the US Army
in Japan shortly after the end of the Second World War. Occupation duty in Japan was very pleasant: the scenery and the women
were beautiful; the climate and the food, good; recreation, communication and transportation facilities, all well developed. Quite
the opposite was true of Korea (with the exception of the women
and the scenery, of course), and the land across the Sea of Japan
came to be looked upon as a kind of soldier's Siberia. The inevitable threat employed by everyone who held command, from
corporal to general, was, "You goof up once more, my friend,
and you can pack your gear for Korea."

A similar attitude towards Afghanistan prevails—or rather it
did a decade ago—amongst the diplomatic corps in Karachi. Third
secretaries who made bad mistakes were threatened with transfer
to Khorramshahr or Aden. Those who were guilty of really
heinous sins were threatened with Kabul. Pakistanis whose fathers
or grandfathers had once been to Kabul told tales of the primitive
physical and insecure social conditions which prevailed in the
remote kingdom. At least two distinguished English authors of
recent years who have written vividly and entrancingly of their
travels through Pakistan have lapsed into grey sullenness when
telling of side trips into Afghanistan.

Conditioned by this background, I was not entirely surprised
when I sought out 'The Royal Afghan Mail' in Peshawar for my
first venture beyond the Khyber. The vehicle was put together—
and none too solidly at that, it appeared—from a lorry chassis and

a square home-made wooden body. A great pile of boxes and bales of the most peculiar sizes and shapes was loaded into and on top of the vehicle before the passengers were permitted to board. There were eleven of us in all: ten Afghans and myself. Two *burqa*-shrouded ladies claimed a narrow seat just behind the driver. The rest of us perched on benches amongst the freight.

It was evident before we left the Kissakhani Bazaar in Peshawar behind us that most of whatever springs there had been in the lorry chassis had been removed. Before we had gone a dozen miles into the Khyber I had banged my head as many times against various unyielding objects, and had decided that the modest price of my ticket to Kabul (less than a pound) had not been such a bargain after all. At the far end of the Khyber it took considerable determination to set down the cup of tea which was provided, as always, at the Pakistani customs-house, and climb back aboard the 'Mail' to set out upon the deeply rutted track which led off across Afghanistan. (Until a couple of years ago the paved road ended precisely on the Durand Line.)

All at once, somehow, the pall lifted. The countryside, with its crumbling mud forts and occasional tiny oasis, had the same stark beauty of the hills on the other side of the border and, to my imagination at least, an added note of the ancient, wild, secretiveness of Central Asia. My aching body began to adjust itself to the jolting of the 'Mail', and the hours that stretched ahead to Kabul did not seem quite so interminable.

Things showed even more promise when a fellow passenger pulled himself around the crate against which I had braced my back and settled himself at my side. He looked like a Hollywood producer's idea of just the man to play opposite Marlene Dietrich in a gypsy film: liquid eyes, hawk nose, warm brown skin, white teeth, and gold ear-rings. He was dressed in patched and faded khaki, the end of his shirt dangling below his knees. On top was an obviously shop new waistcoat of electric blue with vast scrolls of silver embroidery.

By way of greeting, he reached into the inner recesses of his waistcoat and with solemn deliberateness produced a hard-boiled egg. He broke the shell against a crate, peeled the egg, chopped it in two with a typical, heavy-shafted Afghan dagger (also extracted from inside the waistcoat), and offered me half. Next a salt-cellar bearing the emblem of the Great Eastern Hotel appeared, and we also shared that condiment with its peculiar connotation of friendship and brotherhood.

"English bad," he announced, and began rummaging in his waistcoat again. Out came, in turn, a pad of stationery printed with the name 'Dost Mohammad Khan Kabuli' and an address in the currency-exchange bazaar in Calcutta, a snapshot of himself with a Sikh policeman in front of Government House in Calcutta, a receipt for a round trip aeroplane ticket between Calcutta and Peshawar, and a battered Afghan passport. He supplemented these documents with a score of words in English, a dozen in Italian, and four or five in French to make perfectly clear that he was an Afghan money-lender on a visit home from his business in Calcutta.

His *bona fides* established, he got to the point, and, looking around, I became aware that he was representing a number of other passengers as well as himself. Each of them, it appeared, had bought several pairs of Peshawar's famous shoes. In order to avoid duty payments and possible confiscation, they wanted me to take charge of the footwear when we passed through the Afghan customs-stations at Loe Dakka and in the outskirts of Kabul. They assumed, apparently, that the customs-officers, almost always kind to foreigners anyway, would see nothing unusual in one travelling with a single small suitcase and a dozen loose pairs of shoes of varying sizes.

Shoes began to pile up next to me while I considered this doubtful proposition. Abruptly, a decisive female voice emanated from one of the *burqas* at the front of the bus. Her suggestion was considered briefly by the men around me, and then the shoes were rapidly passed up to disappear under the *burqas* of the two ladies. The business at hand conveniently disposed of, we gentlemen had more eggs all around.

We had eggs, and whenever we stopped at the tea-houses beside the road—which was often—we had green tea, bread, and a bit of cheese or a choice *kebab*. Never was I allowed to pay—although I suspected that almost every morsel I ate or drank meant just that much less for some of my obviously impoverished companions. The 'Mail' broke down at about eleven o'clock at night and we waited for five cold hours while the driver and his assistants built a fire and did an improvised weld on the defective part. The only two blankets in the group were pressed upon me and I slept for an hour or so. When I awoke, I found that one of my companions had also added his coat to my covering. All told, it took us twenty-five hours to complete the one-hundred-and-fifty-mile trip between Peshawar and Kabul, and the social side of the business was as delightful as the physical side was discomforting.

The Afghan charm continued to manifest itself in Kabul. It is a big, bustling city clustered around a steep rocky escarpment along the banks of the Kabul River. An ancient rampart, as twisting and battlemented as the Great Wall of China, runs along the ridges. Despite the bustle, motor-vehicles are comparatively rare and animal traffic prevails. When I set out in a *tonga* to find a friend in the American Embassy who had promised to provide a place for me to stay, I was reminded again of the isolation of Kabul, rare amongst the cities of Asia and Africa. My words 'American Embassy' (familiar today in the most unlikely and obscure parts of the World) drew a blank look from the driver. '*L'Ambassade des États Unis*' produced the same response. It was only after I had laboriously constructed the Persian phrase '*Safarat-i-Amerikai*' and tried it out with several different accents that we got under way.

After a bath and a change of clothes, I took myself off to the Press Department where I had been told by Afghan diplomats in London and Karachi I would find help in pursuing my studies. I explained that I was on a Ford Foundation Fellowship studying the Pathans and that I had once been in the American Embassy in Karachi but had never before visited Afghanistan. I indicated my desire to see some people concerned with the tribes and mentioned a few names I had heard, all middle-level officials save one, who was a deputy cabinet-minister. The Press Department promised to see what it could do.

When I returned the next day, the results did not appear to be promising. Three of the officials I had named were on tour; one was ill; and one was out of the country. "We have managed to arrange one appointment for you, though," said the official in charge. "You will see His Royal Highness, the Prime Minister, at 11 a.m. Sunday."

I had heard Prime Minister Sardar Daud Mohammad Khan described as possessing 'ninety per cent of the brains and ninety-five per cent of the guts' in Afghanistan. This is outrageously unfair to the rest of the Afghans, all of whom, including the prime minister's brother, Foreign Minister Prince Naim, and his cousin, King Zahir Shah, are liberally endowed with both intelligence and courage. The description was apt, however, in so far as it emphasised most forcefully the extraordinary energy and determination which is concentrated in the person of the prime minister.

Beneath the quiet graciousness with which the prime minister received me, I detected a restless, smouldering quality more in accord with his long Durrani face, shaven head, and military moustache than with his soft grey suit of British cut. He quickly and accurately sketched the history of the Pathans and their connections with the Sikhs, British India and the Afghan kingdom. Then with a grim smile he said, "And now there is the question of Pushtoonistan . . ."

Daud Mohammad Khan has always been a most vigorous advocate—and indeed some say, the virtual architect—of the Pushtoonistan movement, which demands that the six million Pathans living east of the Durand Line in Pakistan be given the right of self-determination. So vigorous is he in promoting this cause that a few months after my interview with him he made a public speech sufficiently strong to inspire a mob attack on the Pakistani Embassy in Kabul. A year after our talk he called together a *Loe Jirga*, the Grand Assembly of Tribes which discusses the most important public matters and takes place perhaps only once in a generation. The result was a deliberate turning to the USSR to obtain economic and military aid and political support to pursue the Pushtoonistan cause.

None of this had yet happened when we talked in 1954, although even then, of course, the dispute with Pakistan had simmered for seven years—ever since Afghanistan had cast the sole dissenting vote to Pakistan's admission to the United Nations. Daud Mohammad Khan praised Abdul Ghaffar Khan, whom I had met some time earlier in Karachi. Daud's attitude towards 'Pushtoonistan' was somewhat different, however, from that of the leader of the Frontier 'Red Shirts'. While he stressed that Afghanistan had no irredentist claims on the territory of the Pathans east of the Durand Line, he obviously was proudly aware that his ancestors had ruled there less than one hundred and fifty years ago—not long as time is reckoned in that part of the World.

He insisted, simply, that the Pathans in Pakistan were entitled to claim independence if they chose to do so and that the Afghans, as the same people, had the right to promote the Pushtoon cause. In reply to my question as to the probable outcome of a plebiscite, he expressed the belief that a vast majority would prefer independence, and went on to argue for the viability of a separate Pushtoon state, claiming that its creation would end the differences between Afghanistan and Pakistan and make it possible for both countries to provide aid and guidance to the new state.

He agreed with me that holding a plebiscite amongst the tribesmen might be a very difficult thing and suggested that the mechanics by which the Pathans expressed their wishes were not important. "Certainly," he said with a wry grin, "we Pushtoons are not a people who have any great problems about making known our wishes when something concerns us strongly."

Picking this up, I said I wondered how strongly the Pathans in Pakistan were concerned with independence. I had travelled fairly widely on the Frontier, I pointed out, and, except for an occasional whisper (based, I sometimes suspected, as much on love of intrigue as desire for autonomy), I had seen no signs of discontent. He promised me that I should have access to some of the same sources of information as he and his government, and after an hour and a half we parted. I was still not sure just why I had been honoured with ninety minutes of his time, but I knew I had met a man to remember.

A day or so later I was invited to have tea with a number of Pathan *maliks* from the Pakistan side of the Border who were described as leaders of the 'Pushtoonistan' movement. We met in a great stone room in the Ministry of Tribal Affairs. As always, I was struck with the incongruity of the delicately laid tea-table with its fragile china and array of sweet cakes and the bearded, burly men in a variety of tribal clothing who moved around it.

The 'Pushtoonistani' *maliks* were, by and large, an impressive lot. One had been perhaps the most influential *malik* amongst the Afridis before defecting to Kabul. (He has since returned to Pakistan.) Another, a Mohmand, was a distinguished Pushtu poet. A third was widely known in the country inhabited by Pathans in Baluchistan around Fort Sandeman. There was also a lieutenant of the Fakir of Ipi whose name I recalled from its frequent ap-

pearances in villainous rôles in British records of the disturbances
in Waziristan in the Thirties. Most interesting of all, perhaps,
from the standpoint of history, was the brother of the famous
Ajab Khan whose kidnapping of Mollie Ellis some thirty years
earlier has already been described.

They were all fluent, free-spoken men and some of them
seemed remarkably well informed on my activities on the other
side of the international boundary. "Why did you not visit my
village where you would have learned the truth about the way
we are oppressed?" demanded the Afridi. "I will tell you why.
Because your friend, the political agent, would not let you. Well,
I do not let him come there either, but you may come with me
any time you want to."

Ajab Khan's venerable brother glowed with pride and unfolded
some reminiscences after I had told him that his family's exploits
of thirty years before were still remembered in the outside world;
he invited me to visit him at the home he had shared with his
brother near Mazaar-i-Sharif in northern Afghanistan, and then
delivered a carefully phrased complaint to the effect that "The
British we do not mind, but we are hurt that your people who
have fought for their own liberty do not support the cause of
our freedom."

Perhaps I am unfair, but I thought that beneath the dash and
courage which surrounded these old warriors still eager for the
field, there was a note of bitterness and cynicism, in which hurt
pride and petty grievances played as large a rôle as patriotism and
idealism. They did not seem a band of brothers so much as a collection of chieftains in exile, each concerned more with his own
honour and desires than with the ultimate well-being of their
people.

It was a different atmosphere which I found the next day at
the Khushal Khan Khattak School, centre of the younger generation of 'Pushtoonistanis'. The school is situated in a pleasant whitewashed building on the outskirts of Kabul at the foot of the
escarpment which dominates the city. On one side is a delightful
Central Asian garden in which lies the exquisitely simple tomb
of Babur, the first Great Mogul, who directed before his death
in 1530 that his remains should rest in a garden in his beloved
Kabul. A bit farther along are the machine-shops of Jangalak, a
small but thriving industrial settlement, served when I first visited

the place by West German technicians but now under the aegis of Soviet engineers.

The six hundred boys who were at the Khushal Khan School at the time of my visit enjoyed educational facilities which were amongst the best in Afghanistan. Their hostel was neat, clean and attractive. So were their uniforms, a standardised version of tribal dress. Classes were small and books and teaching-aids more in evidence than usual. Subjects covered a wide range, and, as far as I could see, the standard of instruction was far above the average in Asia.

The place was a hot-bed of fervent nationalism. The lithograph maps on the wall showed 'Pushtoonistan' as a separate entity, encompassing all the territory between the Indus River and the Durand Line, from the Himalayas to the Arabian Sea. The language of instruction was Pushtu. History and literature classes emphasised the rich heritage of the Pushtuns. The 'Pushtoonistan' flag flew in the schoolyard. The songs the boys sang for me were anthems of Pushtun freedom. The games they played were set in the context of a war for independence.

They were a bright, eager, cheerful lot, given to boyish sky-larking when the rein of school discipline was relaxed a little because of the presence of a visitor. Yet, on the subject of 'Pushtoonistan', they were fanatically devoted to their cause and to each other—a condition one always finds a little disquieting in the young. To them, 'Pushtoonistan' was both a reality and an ideal. They burned to serve it and to emulate the glory of their ancestors by cutting down any and all who stood in its way.

While the boys were lining up for the roll-call in the schoolyard, I asked the principal where most of them were from: Pakistan or Afghanistan? "Pushtoonistan," he said with a smile, and directed that they should call out their village or district when replying to their names on the roll. I did not recognise all the names, but a good many certainly were from tribal territory on the Pakistani side of the Durand Line.

Back in Pakistan later I asked a number of tribesmen if any of their sons were in the Khushal Khan School. Several who were obviously loyal to Pakistan admitted readily that they had sons or grandsons there. "Why? It is simple. The political agent knows," explained one. "These people from Kabul come down here and say that they will educate our sons free. There may not be enough places in our own school sometimes, so we let them go. We know what kind of a place the Khushal Khan School is, but it costs them much time and money to educate our boys, and is it not a clever thing to let them spend all that on our people who despise them? When our sons come back we will laugh together at their stupidity."

How clever it is, I am not sure. The Pathans know their own sons better than I do, but I cannot help wondering how well filial devotion and clan ties hold up after several years of massive cultural indoctrination—especially when the subject of indoctrination has a genuine romantic and idealistic appeal of its own and those who are exposed to it lack the wisdom and experience of the battle-scarred *maliks* with whom I shared tea, who view 'Pushtoonistan' according to a more cynical and traditional set of rules.

The Pathans, after all, constitute something less than half the total population of Afghanistan, and there is much more to Kabul than just 'Pushtoonistan'. The people in the streets are, perhaps, even a bit more colourful and cosmopolitan than they are in Peshawar. The colder climate accounts at least in part for this. For much of the year a man needs an outer garment; in Kabul his choice for this is wide indeed. The *chogha*, a commodious, ankle-length, half overcoat, half cloak, is available in dozens of styles and colours and degrees of decrepitude. The faces of the people are equally varied: Hazaras, with the slant eyes and wispy beards of their Mongol ancestors; swaggering Pathans, often with blue eyes and the fairest of skin; the delicate, finely featured faces of Tajiks and Kabulis of Persian ancestry. There is a heavy sprinkling of uniforms: army officers in sharply styled khaki wool with red collar tabs reminiscent of Chinese Nationalists; enlisted men with puttees of seemingly Japanese design and with peaked caps, also vaguely Japanese, on their shaven heads; and, most common of all, police in high black boots, light purple breeches, faded pinkish jackets and tall peaked caps.

The buildings in the business section—at least the older ones—have a style all their own. One street reminded me more than anything else of the ancient photographs I have seen of Russian villages in Alaska a hundred years back. In the residential areas everything is surrounded by long high walls. Walking down the streets, one gets a peculiarly acute sense of the traditional secretive-

ness of Kabul. Nothing is to be seen save the rutted road running
between blank walls pierced here and there by small wooden
gates. To travel about the streets by foot or *tonga* at night is a
reckless matter, for the ruts are deep and are often half filled with
the overflow from the open sewers which run by the side of the
road. A stumble into one of them is an experience relished by
neither horse nor man.

During my first visit there was only one paved street, and that
scarcely a block long. When Khrushchev and Bulganin came a
year later, the main streets on which they travelled were metalled
by the growing crew of Soviet technicians. Now more streets
are paved and Soviet-made taxis and buses run about all over the
city. Despite all the asphalt and concrete which has been put down,
one thing has remained the same. Dust is everywhere, lying in a
light frosting on the clothes of the people, resting in a heavy
mantle on the walls and roofs of the buildings, and hanging in
great clouds in the shimmering air between the city and the
mountains which surround it.

There have been other and more significant changes, of course.
Not the least of these has concerned women, a subject avoided as
carefully in Kabul as on the Frontier in the old days.

In the 1920s, when the young King Amanulla was trying
rapidly and forcefully to drag his kingdom out of the medieval
into the modern age, many Afghan women put aside their *burqas*,
or *chaudris* as they are called in Afghanistan, and went to school
and appeared in public with their men. Then in 1929 came the
revolt which overthrew Amanulla, sparked off in large part by
charges from religious and tribal conservatives that the new
customs were a profanation of Islam. When order was finally re-
established the new regime, headed by the uncles and father of
King Zahir and the Princes Daud and Naim, took the lesson to
heart. They proceeded slowly with modernisation in many
spheres, but the high-heeled slippers and Paris gowns disappeared
once again under *chaudris* and the women were relegated to a
seclusion more severe than ever before. In 1955 only those men
whose memories reached back more than a quarter of a century
had ever seen an unveiled Afghan woman on the streets of Kabul.

Five years later the picture was very different. Out near Babur's
tomb, the swimming-pool which Amanulla had built for his
officials and their wives was still crumbling and unused, as was

the shuttered derelict building of the 'Café Shah Babur' on the terrace above, designed as a summer restaurant for eating and dancing. The Afghan Airlines plane which had brought me to Kabul, however, had a trim and efficient stewardess of an influential Durrani family. In the streets about every third woman walked quietly but proudly unveiled. The change has been due largely to the indomitable determination of Prince Daud, who, having decided that the time was ripe to try again, did so with his usual force. Government officials were told that their wives and daughters should appear in public and that they should even take employment in jobs where they could contribute to the progress of their country. This time the opposition from religious sources had been effectively controlled, and one has the feeling that there is a new element in this reform, at once more moderate and more lasting than before.

Ironically, the change has merely added fuel to the flames of controversy between Afghanistan and Pakistan. Many of the more traditionally-minded Pathans in Pakistan object to the new Afghan mode, denouncing it as a violation of Islam enforced by the 'godless Russians' who are now so prominent in Afghanistan. The Afghans in turn point to the gay hotels of Karachi where beautiful women in gay and colourful clothes are a commonplace. And so, of course, the quarrel goes on.

Let me leave the Pathans behind for a moment. I have been lucky almost every time I have visited Kabul in that I have been able to see one of the games of *buskashi*, which are held on occasions of national celebration or rejoicing. *Buskashi* has its origin north of the Hindu Kush Mountains and few Pathans play the game, though they are as eager spectators as everyone else.

Buskashi is played by two teams on horseback who struggle against each other for possession of the carcass of a sheep—usually soaked in water and weighing about one and a half hundredweight. These are the only constants in the game, and by and large there are no rules. Such conventions as are desirable on a given occasion are determined by the number of men and the amount of space available at the time.

In Kabul Stadium the teams seem to run sixteen to twenty a side, and the specific object of the game is for one team to pick up the dead sheep from a hole at one end of the field and carry it, passing it to team-mates when necessary, around a pole at the other end of the field and back to deposit it in the hole again. The carcass must be picked up while the player is in the saddle and while the members of the other team are doing all they can to prevent its getting off the ground.

Merely riding with the sheep on the tiny Badakhshani ponies without being pulled from the saddle by its weight is no mean trick. Doing so while almost a score of opposing players are trying to cut the rider with their whips, drag him from his mount, or trip the beast itself, requires extraordinary strength and skill. When the sheep is on the ground, as it is most of the time, thirty-odd horsemen may mill around it for ten minutes or more, beating each other with whips and charging their ponies into the middle of the mêlée, literally over the backs of men and horses in front of them. Every minute or so a riderless horse emerges from the scramble and then eventually a man is dragged out or crawls out himself from beneath the ponies' legs to go off to have his head or limbs repaired. The ponies seem to enjoy it as much as the men and are as vigorous in their biting and kicking of each other.

There is a kind of rough team-play to be discerned as one team passes the sheep amongst its members and blocks out opposing players, but to the eye of the non-professional spectator, at least, it appears to be mostly every man for himself. The players, generally Uzbeks and Tajiks from the North, wear high-heeled boots every bit as colourful as those of American cowboys. The rest of the costume is even more flamboyant: turbans or small gold pillar-box hats on their heads, padded jackets with the emblem of their team, streaming cummerbunds and baggy trousers. One would think that if ever there was a 'young man's game' buskashi would be it, but many of the most able players are greybeards.

There are usually one or two referees on the field; incongruously, they wear English riding-clothes, but I have never been able to see that they had any significant affect on the progress of the game. The signal to begin and the final decision in the Kabul Stadium games is given by the King. After every score both teams thunder up to rein in at the foot of the royal box, each shouting for a decision in its favour. The losers always demand another round, no matter what the original arrangement may have been.

The stadium is an oval with about a dozen huge stone steps running all the way around. Each of these is three or four feet high and the onlookers dispose themselves on the stones at random. There is no 'off-side' and I have seen the game going on as high as the third and fourth steps with thirty wildly excited horses and their riders churning in the middle of the spectators. At other times the whole band will be strung out in a gallop across the field, whips flailing and riders leaning half-way out of their saddles as they try to bring down the man racing along with the sheep.

The last *buskashi* game which I saw was in early winter when the Paghman Range, which surmounts the horizon opposite the stadium with a massive saw-toothed line of its own, was already solid white with snow. The sun shone orange-red through the dust haze above the valley floor; it obscured the telephone-lines strung out beyond the stadium and threw a concealing shadow over the bright modernity of the King's limousine parked near the royal box. The blood and flame of the late afternoon light glowed strongly on the horsemen racing back and forth on their ponies tearing at a torn sheep, blood from whip cuts streaming down many of their faces. The barbaric living frieze would have delighted Timur-i-Lang, and once caught in the mind of any man, it is not soon forgotten.

However exotic are the people of the North, one cannot remain for long unaware of the Pushtuns in Afghanistan. Whether they call themselves Afghans, Pathans, Durranis, Afridis, Wazirs or something else, the country, as its name indicates, is theirs. They rule it; their interests are its interests; their language and culture are coming more and more to replace the traditional Persian. (The latter, incidentally, is still the real mother tongue of many of the most influential Durrani families—even though their blood lines and customs are Pushtun.)

The subject of 'Pushtoonistan' is never far beneath the surface. Some of its manifestations are unpleasant, as in the intense and deliberate promotion in the Khushal Khan School of an extreme pride of race in a people whose confidence of their own superiority has been virtually unparalleled for centuries. In a country where the sources of news are limited, the press and radio trumpet the cause until it must grate a little in the ears of all but its most fanatic devotees. All of this, of course, as well as occasional counterblasts of propaganda from Pakistan, contributes to the further embitterment of relations between two neighbouring states which certainly have far more in common than most states in the modern World. This, I think it can be said without questioning the motives of either party, is extremely unfortunate.

All in all, I can only conclude that the celebrated Afghan charm wears well. The country is as interesting and as hospitable as a visitor can find anywhere. Such stratification as there is in Afghan society is largely economic. Courtesy, wit and courage are the common heritage of all classes, and in the virtues that most become a free man, the princely prime minister and the vagabond money-lender are one. In this sense both of them are also one with the Pathans of Pakistan who, I think on this point at least, would happily agree.

XVII

The Pathan Tomorrow

IN THE CHAPTERS that have gone before, I have tried to represent the Pathans as best I could from their own point of view. After all, as is the case with most of us, to a considerable extent they are what they think they are. Now, in the compulsive way of the West, I propose to take a brief look at what the future may hold for the Frontier. In doing so it is necessary to step aside and take the rôle of a third party, for most Pathans think little of tomorrow. At least, they think little in the gloomy, cosmic way which has become a habit in the West since the advent of nuclear-weapons, intercontinental missiles, and the race for the control of space.

Why this should be is not easy to say. It is not from lack of knowledge. Even the most remote tribal villages are likely to have a battery radio and the tribesmen are generally remarkably well informed on World events. It is not a case of 'Eat, drink, and be merry . . .', for the Pathans are anything but hedonists; when they think of death it is likely to be that of their enemies rather than their own. Certain specific 'tomorrows' are real enough, of course; revenge in Kashmir, a good crop, the advantageous marriage of a son or daughter.

Partly, I suppose, the reason for the lack of general interest in the future lies in acute awareness of a glorious past and a satisfactory present; partly it comes from Islamic fatalism which sees the events of tomorrow, as well as those of today and yesterday, as the will of Allah; partly it grows out of the importance in a Pathan's life of honour—a timeless concept.

Yet, of course, the Pathans will be affected by tomorrow, both in their own way of life and in the rôle they and their land are called upon to play in the broader context of World affairs.

To touch on the latter first, the land of the Pathans is still the gateway to South Asia and the Indian Ocean. If new military tactics have rendered obsolete and amusing the tank traps in the

Khyber and the Kurrum, tactics may change again and give them back their usefulness. Even if they do not, political geography has not changed, and the capture of the Pathans by propaganda or subversion would be just as great a defeat for free men as conquest of them by force. Happily, neither event seems very likely at the moment, yet we should not forget that the "grey-coat guard on the Helmund ford" which Kipling feared three-quarters of a century ago and the smooth Pushtu tones emanating from Radio Tashkent today represent similar threats.

'The Great Game' which Britain played with imperial Russia did not end with the Bolshevik Revolution. There is ample evidence in the public record to show that Soviet agents were busy in Afghanistan in the years after the First World War. There are Pathans to be met on the Frontier today who served with the British intervention force in Baku in 1918. There are others who attended the notorious Soviet espionage school in Tashkent and the 'University of the Toilers of the East' in Moscow. In the Twenties and Thirties, the British administration in India charged the Soviets with responsibility for tribal uprisings and at times suspected—erroneously, I think—Abdul Ghaffar Khan and his 'Red Shirts' of links with the Soviet Union.

The intrigue faded out during the Second World War when British India and the USSR were allies in a common cause, and there was relative calm for a few years after the war. In 1947, when Britain withdrew from the Indian subcontinent, everyone knew that a far-reaching change in the power balance of the area was occurring. Yet, the lull in 'the Great Game' continued a few years longer. Soon Soviet pressure in Asia was manifested again in the Korean War; with that ominous lesson in mind, Pakistan began to seek ways to promote its own security. With the unity of the subcontinent rent by the many quarrels with India growing out of the Partition, and Prime Minister Nehru firmly embarked on a policy of neutralism in the international field, the answer came in the Baghdad Pact (now CENTO, the Central Treaty Organisation) and SEATO (the South-East Asia Treaty Organisation). These alliances brought closer bilateral ties with the United States and an increasing flow of American economic and military aid.

Afghanistan faced problems also. The withdrawal of British power from the subcontinent destroyed Afghanistan's classic rôle

S NISHTceu

as the buffer state between two great powers. Even if this had not been so, the fervour for political and economic development which was sweeping the rest of Asia was touching the remote kingdom with an unsettling finger. If security were to be maintained and the foreign aid essential for development obtained, a new policy was necessary. Besides, of course, there was the problem of 'Pushtoonistan'.

Kabul made tentative overtures to the West in the early 1950s, hoping, one suspects, for a solution to its problems somewhat like that which Pakistan had found. This was not to be, however. The country's proximity to the USSR, its remoteness from the power centres of the West, and its deep-seated quarrel with Pakistan (and to a lesser degree with Persia) were too great obstacles. Afghanistan turned then, beginning about 1954, to the USSR for economic, military and political assistance. Ever since the Soviet presence in Afghanistan has grown. The Afghans have proceeded with their traditional caution in dealing with the Russians and modest, though by no means insignificant, lines have been kept open to the West. Just how much influence Moscow has achieved in the country is a subject for endless argument amongst diplomats and commentators both inside and outside of Afghanistan. Certainly, it is more than the Afghans would like and less than the Soviets want.

These developments, of course, have not passed unnoticed by the Pathans. The USSR has supported Afghanistan on the 'Pushtoonistan' question and India on the Kashmir issue. CENTO and SEATO and the Western allies have stood firm on the validity of the Durand Line. China, intent on drawing its own line in the Himalayas, has undertaken a concentrated agitation of the question of the present undefined boundary, moving its pressure steadily westward from India's North-East Frontier Agencies, through Nepal, Bhutan, Sikkim, Ladakh and Kashmir, in the direction of Pakistan's Gilgit and Afghanistan's Wakhan.

To make sure that no one who is interested misses these events, Radio Moscow broadcasts them in Persian, Pushtu, Urdu and English. The British Broadcasting Corporation and the Voice of America beam out their own versions in several languages. Radio Kabul is on the air daily in Persian, Pushtu, Russian and English; Radio Pakistan, in Persian, Urdu, Pushtu and English. The last two organisations add to the international complexities their own conflicting pleas for Pushtun superiority on the one hand and the integration of the Pushtuns into the national life on the other.

Even if all the radios in the Frontier villages which bring in this multi-lingual chorus were suddenly to be silent, the Pathans still have their own sharp eyes. They have watched Soviet technicians at work on irrigation projects in the Jelalabad Valley and Canadian engineers working under Colombo Plan auspices throwing a great dam across the river at Warsak on the edge of the Peshawar Valley. Unless my geography is badly awry, there are hills in the Border range upon which a tribesman can stand and merely by turning his head see the con trails of the American-built jets of the Pakistani Air Force in the sky to the east and those of the Soviet-built fighters and bombers of the Royal Afghan Air Force above the western horizon.

As other men, the Pathans react to these sights and sounds according to their individual interests and beliefs. Those who are loyal to Pakistan welcome endorsement of the Durand Line by CENTO and SEATO and are reassured by the new power of their armed forces. Those who favour the 'Pushtoonistan' cause are gratified by Mr Khrushchev's support for their position and see greater strength for it in the Soviet training and equipment which are transforming the Afghan forces. Naturally all this has had its affect on the relative positions and policies of Pakistan and Afghanistan, and it has added in the past few years to the bitterness of their quarrel.

Personally, however, I very much doubt whether it has as yet at least had any great impact on many Pathans' fundamental ideas of their own capacity and destiny. They are not unaware of the possibilities for another Korea or another Laos implicit in their situation. But unlike some other peoples of the under-developed World, they certainly do not look upon themselves as pawns in a battle between the great powers. As far as I can see, they are no less sure now than they ever were of their ability to determine their own destiny and to use the more powerful and sophisticated elements of the World for their own ends. This, I think, is another reason why they sometimes seem relatively little concerned with the future.

When I try to stand aside, as I promised in the beginning of this chapter, to consider objectively the future of the Frontier, I find myself, I fear, less confident. It appears unlikely that in these critical times the Pathans can continue indefinitely to ignore or to defy forces to which even the great nations of the World must bend. Nevertheless, this is what, through courage and determination, they have succeeded in doing many times in the past. And, of course, these forces, as global and compelling as they are, sometimes change.

For example, there is, I think, still hope for a solution of the 'Pushtoonistan' issue—despite more than a dozen years of past recriminations and the likelihood of more to come. To the casual observer in Pakistan, India and Afghanistan appear to be twin enemies, Kashmir and 'Pushtoonistan', twin injuries. Yet, as one studies these matters more closely, important differences begin to appear.

Pakistan and India fear each other in a deep atavistic way. Many Pakistanis suspect that India has never accepted the fact of the Partition and hopes one day to reunite the subcontinent under Hindu rule. Many Indians, on the other hand, are acutely aware of the long history of Muslim conquest based in the north-west portion of the subcontinent; others find the idea of religious unity which underlay the foundation of Pakistan a threat to their own goal of a secular state. These attitudes are not universal; they can and indeed are being overcome. However, for a long time to come they will make difficult the development of real trust and understanding between the two countries, and whatever political accommodations are reached are likely to come only after cautious and prolonged negotiations.

The attitudes underlying relations between Pakistan and Afghanistan are different. Both peoples have a common religious and cultural heritage. Neither would destroy the other, if it could. There is little hatred or fear between them, although each seems to get a high degree of satisfaction out of antagonising the other. Their relationship is less that of strangers or enemies than that of proud and irascible brothers. The latter, of course, especially when a touch of jealousy is thrown in, can be deadly indeed. Nevertheless the feeling of kinship is there, and even when relations are at their most bitter, neither side seems altogether happy at having to seek support against the other from its great-power allies. Indeed, many leaders and officials on both sides remain able to contemplate with equanimity and even with hope the prospect of some kind of eventual confederation of their two countries.

At best this is a long way off, and some solution to the 'Push-toonistan' problem is obviously a prerequisite even to an improvement in relations. Many forms of settlement of this thorny issue have been proposed; it is idle to debate them here, save to say that I personally believe that something will one day be worked out. If it is, Pakistan, Afghanistan and their Pathans will have taken a step which will change profoundly the nature of 'the Great Game' in their part of the World. In so far as the change would involve the elimination of dissension amongst free men and the promotion of their development and integration, the West, at least, could regard it with a benign eye.

There is room also for speculation about the future of the Pathans and their way of life in their own hills and plains. One of the reasons for their strength and independence is that their tribal society is still dynamic and flexible within its long-established framework. But it is, of course, being subjected to increasing pressures from the outside—social and economic, as well as political.

The radio broadcasts which are beamed at the Frontier may concentrate on political matters, but necessarily they also bring to the Pathans' isolated world an increasing consciousness of other things: the existence of 'haves' and 'have-nots' in the Modern World, the ample opportunities for entertainment, and the great flow of consumer-goods which have burgeoned in the prosperous years after the Second World War. This, supplemented by the taste of the good life which Pakistan has for some years provided through the extension of welfare and medical services, could hardly help but bring a whiff of the winds of change into the most remote villages of the hills.

The deposing of the nawab of Dir and the occupation and administration of Bajaur by the Pakistan Government in 1960 consummated a series of political and administrative changes designed to reduce—and presumably eventually to eliminate—the special status of tribal territory. As such, it is certainly a major milestone in the social and political history of the Frontier. In any event, there can be little doubt that the outside World does not intend to leave the Pathans alone as much in the future as has been the case in the past.

Many observers are convinced that the intrusion of modern civilisation into the Frontier will have the same affect it has had in most other parts of Asia, Africa and Latin America: detribalisation, permanent settlement, increasing urbanisation, and a greater likelihood of susceptibility to radical political and economic ideas.

As was obvious in the first chapter of this book, my own introduction to the Frontier took place in a romantic mood instilled by the influence of Kipling and a long-standing taste for exotica. It was not long, however, before I began to see the other side of Pathan life. All the tribesmen, and especially the weaker ones, the women and the children, lead a hard life. Tuberculosis and malaria are not glamorous afflictions when one sees the bloodied lips or shaking limbs of a friend. Close up, the machinations of politicians, whether tribal *maliks* or the leaders of political parties, are seldom edifying. A widow weeping over the body of her murdered husband is not a pleasant sight, even if he has been dispatched from the highest motives of honour. Impoverished, ignorant, and diseased children are a blot on any society.

If this book had been written a year or two after my first meeting with the Pathans, it would have contained much more of this seamy side of life on the Frontier. That such things do not loom large in the present work is not, I hope, proof that I am an incurable romantic unable to see the reality behind Khushal Khan Khattak's stirring poems and Kipling's glorious images. It is simply that, as I have got to know the Pathans even a little, I have found a deep love of freedom and respect for the dignity of the individual which has produced a willingness to subordinate physical and even spiritual comfort to preserve more basic values. This is true not only of the isolated hillsman but of the most worldly and sophisticated Pathan.

I have never met amongst the Pathans that unfortunately common figure amongst Asians and Africans: the unhappy and maladjusted man caught half-way between his own culture and that of the West. I have, however, met *émigré* Pathans selling real-estate in California, renovating houses in London, playing expert bridge for profit on transatlantic liners, and happily and competently engaged in a score of other professions never dreamed of when they scampered up and down the barren hills of their boyhood. I have also met Pathans sitting in traditional dress in their *hujras* talking quietly of crops, marriages and feuds, until the proper time came to relish the amazement of the Western visitor when they slip casually into a discussion of the relative merits of various London tailors, Paris restaurants, and Roman museums.

It is in this urbane flexibility worn charmingly over an iron will and a hard core of principle that a clue to the future of the Pathans may be found. In the regulation of their affairs, the shot in the night may give way to the ballot in the box. Government-supplied schools, hospitals, and irrigation-canals may succeed the subsidies which long ago succeeded the caravan raids; the tribesmen may even one day become, like all of us, taxpayers.

Yet, unless the Pathans forget in a generation a thousand years of tradition and the *mores* of a tribal society still very much alive, they will cast their ballots, study in their schools, and pay their taxes with the same strength of character and according to the same set of values. This is another reason, or perhaps the same one, why the Pathans appear little concerned for their future. I, for one, think they can afford to be so.

Index